The Only LLC Beginner's Guide You'll Ever Need

Limited Liability Companies For Beginners - Form, Manage & Maintain Your LLC

By

Garrett Monroe

Buyer Bonus

As a way of saying thank you for your purchase, we're offering three FREE downloads that are exclusive to our book readers!

First, The Start Your LLC Checklist that shows you exactly how to get your LLC up and running right away.

Second, The 5 Mistakes Beginners Make When Opening an LLC email course. This will help you avoid costly mistakes when getting started.

And finally, The 7 Best Websites for Starting Your LLC PDF that'll save you tons of hours of researching so you can get your LLC going today.

Inside all these bonuses, you'll discover:

- The top 3 states to start your LLC to give it the best chance of success, and most tax advantages.

- All your LLC questions answered so you can get it going with zero confusion.

- The top 7 websites to start your LLC ranked, with pros and cons for each, so you can easily choose the best one for your situation.

- The #1 mistake beginners make that can doom your LLC before you even make your first sale (and how to avoid it).

- All this, and much more…

To download your bonuses, you can go to www.LLCLegend.com or simply scan the QR code below:

Table of Contents

The Only LLC Beginner's Guide You'll Ever Need

You want to start a business…or even grow your current one to the next level.

Simple enough, right? You find a problem in a market that people need solved… and you solve it. That is the very foundation of any solid business. And the better you are at solving that problem, the more customers you can get!

But what trips many people up is all the legal jargon that comes with starting a business. And that's the situation Jake found himself in. Maybe you can relate.

Jake recently quit his job to start his own business after years of being stuck in a job he hated. He was ready to immerse himself in the design world and enrich people's lives with beautiful graphic designs. He knows a limited liability company ("LLC") will offer him asset protection. However, he's overwhelmed by the complex nature of forming an LLC.

Jake wonders if this is the right move or if he should settle for a sole proprietorship. His business mentor strongly advised him that an LLC was the best move if he wanted to use his money, save on taxes, and protect his assets. As he started the formation process, he hit a roadblock, and now Jake is wondering whether he will succeed in running a business if he cannot figure out how to start an LLC.

As established business owners, we have experienced what Jake is going through. And if you are in the initial stages of starting a business, you could face the same frustrations. For a beginner, LLC formation can seem overwhelming and cause anxiety. You may worry that you are making an expensive legal mistake. The tax rules, business regulations, and legal requirements can make you feel stuck and unable to fulfill your long-awaited dream.

But what if you could simplify the formation process? What if you had a beginner's guidebook that explains the entire process from beginning to end? A book that uses simple English to break down the information you need to successfully establish a legal and functional LLC?

The book in your hands accomplishes this task with precision. "The Only LLC Beginner's Guide You'll Ever Need" promises to show you the right path to take to set up and operate your LLC faultlessly. Here's some of what you'll learn:

- The low-down on sole proprietorships, partnerships, corporations, and cooperatives so you can confirm you're making the right move in choosing an LLC.

- Detailed breakdowns of the formation process. Whether choosing a business name or filing documents with the relevant state institutions, we've got you covered.

- A simple explanation of all the legal, business, and financial concepts and requirements so you don't miss any important steps.

- All the documents you need at every stage, ensuring you leave no legal stone unturned.

- Crucial information about taxation, record keeping, operating agreements, and maintaining LLC status.

- Common operational and legal pitfalls that some LLCs grapple with, eventually leading to the loss of their status.

- Advice on expansion and action you must take to open branches in another location or state. We will help you craft a blueprint for growth and build a winning team.

- All the steps to take if a member wants to exit or you decide to sell or close down the LLC.

- Case studies of how business owners succeed in building an empire after following all the information provided in this guide.

You can be sure this information is factual, reliable, and drawn from experience. Under the pen name Garrett Monroe, we are a team of writers in our 40s with varied business experience from multiple industries, including sales, Artificial Intelligence (AI), real estate, business coaching, and accounting. We've brought together our wealth of experience to help you succeed in your business endeavor.

If you want to operate a legitimate business while protecting your assets, this book is for you. Don't struggle in the dark for longer than you should. Interact with the content in this book and let your dreams become a reality. You can form an LLC without stressing out and still preserve a considerable portion of your capital to set up shop. What's the first step for you? Grab a copy of "The Only LLC Beginner's Guide You'll Ever Need" and begin your transformative journey. You'll gain insider strategies and tips it took us years to perfect. This information is now yours for the taking. Flip the pages and start building your business empire the right way.

Chapter 1

Unlocking the LLC: Your Blueprint to Business Freedom

"Great companies start because the founders want to change the world…not make a fast buck."

-Guy Kawasaki

Starting a business is an adventure that can either be worth the time and effort or leave you feeling drained and with empty pockets. An LLC is a legal structure that enables your entrepreneurial journey to take advantage of key provisions lacking in the other legal structures. As you read this chapter, you will learn what an LLC entails, if it's right for your startup, and the benefits you will enjoy. Before jumping into LLCs, let's explore the other four business structures.

The Fab Four: Business Entities You Need to Know About

As you start your business, the first step is deciding which business structure suits your needs. To ensure you are making the right move in choosing an LLC, we will briefly discuss the four types of business entities under which you can register your business. Being familiar with each entity's main features and tradeoffs will help you pick one that aligns with your circumstances and goals.

Each business structure offers a unique feature that caters to various entrepreneurial needs. Imagine these structures as different pathways leading to the same destination but with varied adventures and challenges along the way. As you read along, have in mind your business identity, financial position, legal footprint, and the people involved.

Sole Proprietorship

A sole proprietorship is the simplest structure to form because you own and run the business as an individual. You have total control of the company and your profits, but you also face unlimited personal liability. When a legal issue arises, or a creditor seeks a pending debt, you may need to pay using your personal possessions.

A sole proprietorship is simple to set up and has minimal paperwork. You only need to obtain permits and licenses that suit your business and location. Fortunately, you do not need to submit formation documents like an LLC or corporation. The simplicity of the starting procedures makes a sole proprietorship a good starting point for new business owners.

New business owners who are aware of the available options shy away from forming a sole proprietorship because they will be responsible for all the management duties and day-to-day work. You also absorb all the risks. Further, your income passes through your personal tax return, and you'll still pay self-employment tax on your business's profit.

If you are starting a simple business with low liability risk, then sole proprietorship is worth considering. But if you plan to take on debt and add employees within a short time, a corporation or LLC may be the better choice.

Partnership

A partnership permits two or more people to share business ownership. As they conduct business, the income and losses flow through to all partners' tax returns. To make it less strenuous to do business together, the partners draft a partnership agreement outlining:

- Profit-sharing

- Responsibilities

- Decision-making

- Ownership stakes

Having a written partnership agreement explaining the various roles and powers reduces the number of disagreements when making big or small decisions. Additional guidelines that should be included in the agreement are procedures for adding new partners, buying out partners, and resolving conflicts.

Notably, general partnerships do not require formal registration with your state to function legally. You can formulate your partnership business structure as you see fit. The ease of this setup makes partnership the go-to option for people who need to merge ideas and resources to succeed in starting a business.

Corporation

Corporations have several unique features that make them stand out from the other business structures. The most outstanding one is that it exists as a separate legal entity from the owners and shareholders. This feature protects you from personal liability for the corporation's legal issues and debts that don't go beyond your investment.

Corporations also have ownership shares that you can transfer to interested parties through buying and selling stock. This feature makes it easy to raise capital and allows shareholders to freely trade their shares.

The main disadvantage that corporations face is double taxation. Your business profits are taxed at the corporate and dividend levels. To a greater extent, this feature cancels out the liability protection and fundraising advantage corporations offer.

Another downside to corporations is that they come with more complicated reporting and record-keeping requirements than sole proprietorships, partnerships, and LLCs. You are required to [1]:

- Hold shareholder and director meetings.

- Keep accurate corporate minutes.

- File annual reports.

- Comply with the state regulations.

If you are just starting a business, forming a corporation often doesn't make financial and legal sense. But as your company grows and you need to attract outside investment, you may benefit from a corporate structure.

Cooperative

In a cooperative, members come together to form, own, and govern the business. They become equal members in profit sharing and decision-making. The co-op members have equal voting rights in deciding major issues because they collectively own the enterprise.

Its unique feature is that members receive the earnings gained in the form of patronage dividends rather than having shareholders from the general public. In addition, members receive special discounts on services and products.

A cooperative offers new business owners a competitive edge because it empowers them to compete with large competitors by gaining established market share, which increases their bargaining power. Some drawbacks that may make you shy away from joining a cooperative is the democratic structure that creates challenges such as:

- Slow decision-making process

- Members prefer short-term over long-term financial benefits

- Reliance on volunteer partnership by members

If you are starting a business in a highly competitive field such as agriculture, utilities, food retailing, healthcare, or financial services, joining a cooperative may be suitable to avoid facing the competition on your own. However, you need to choose one with strong processes because the complex governance structure can slow your growth and limit revenue gains.

There you have it. These are the four business structures you need to know about as we dive into talking about LLCs. Any choice you make from the four structures above or LLC will impact everything, from your financial obligation to personal liability, relationship with partners or shareholders, and capacity for growth.

Is an LLC The Way to Go?

As established business owners from various industries, we can confidently say "Yes," an LLC is the right way to go in many cases. Arguably, an LLC combines the best of both worlds in terms of financial safety. It provides liability protection, has a customizable management structure, offers attractive taxation options, and makes you more credible to potential customers and investors. Let's expand on these game-changing features.

Understanding Liability

No one wants to plan for failure, but the truth is many small businesses and startups don't survive long–term. There are no guarantees of success when starting a business. So, you should protect your personal assets to have your possessions remaining if the business fails. An LLC guarantees that protection as opposed to partnerships or sole proprietorships.

In these structures, creditors can pursue your savings, car, house, or other possessions to get their money back. LLCs successfully prevent this by shielding you from liability. In an LLC, your business exists as a separate entity, and your creditors cannot come after your personal assets if you lose a lawsuit or default on loans.

That said, the liability protection LLCs offer has limitations. For instance, if members do not adhere to all legal formalities or commit fraud, the court overrides this rule and may touch their possessions. In addition, each member directly responsible for injury, harm, or damage remains personally liable for their own negligent actions.

As an illustration, Matt and his four friends established an LLC for outdoor adventures. One summer, Matt leads a hiking tour and fails to secure a client properly, resulting in an injury. In this situation, the LLC shields his friends' personal assets from liability. However, if the court concludes that Matt was grossly negligent and found liable for the injuries, his personal possessions may be used to cover the injury costs.

Management Made Easy

For a startup business, having an outside force like the state dictate how you run and manage your business wouldn't work in your best interest. An LLC provides flexibility in decision-making authority and structuring management, whether you run a manager-managed or member-managed LLC.

In manager-managed LLCs, members appoint qualified managers to oversee day-to-day operations while the rest focus on developing new strategies to grow the business or plan for the future. In member-managed LLCs, all members participate equally in running and managing the business. Decision-making power is often based on majority vote or consensus. This approach keeps all members engaged, but it may also lead to conflict if the guidelines aren't clear.

LLCs also give you more freedom in allocating profit and losses than partnerships. Members do not have to split everything equally but according to a set of criteria like:

- Time investment

- Financial contribution

- Sweat equity

- Business generated by each member

Being able to customize your profit sharing and management authority is a benefit you can't afford to overlook. As you create the operating document, ensure you outline everything and treat it as a constitution that guides all aspects of your business.

Pass-through Taxation

Pass-through taxation is one of the primary reasons most entrepreneurs choose LLCs over corporations and it means your profits and losses pass through the business and go directly to individual members. This provision avoids double taxation corporations go through at the corporate and individual dividend levels. This feature minimizes admin work and ensures all members are taxed once, promoting financial efficiency and maximizing your earnings.

LLCs also offer owners the ability to offset business losses against an income earned outside the business on personal tax. For example, if you have a salaried job that gives you $100,000, and your LLC business loses $30,000 in one year - the law allows you to subtract the $30,000 from the wage income on your personal tax return. As a result, the total amount taxable drops from $100,000 to $70,000, leading to considerable tax savings.

As a budding entrepreneur trying to establish yourself, the pass-through taxation allows you to save money and redirect these resources to other areas, such as expanding services or hiring talent.

Credibility & Longevity

When you register a business as an LLC, it becomes a separate legal entity and removes your personal identity from it. As a result, lenders, vendors, and clients may take your business more seriously, knowing

you have followed legal procedures permitting you to conduct business.

Registering a business as an LLC makes building business credit in your company's name relatively easy. You can apply for credit, open bank accounts, and establish payment histories on your company's employer identification number (EIN) instead of your social security number—making you more credible.

An LLC structure promotes longevity because the company does not dissolve when a member departs, like in partnerships. Ownership interest can be sold or transferred. Further, creditors cannot force a dissolution through the court even if the business struggles with its resources. This increases the chances of your company's survival past the financial challenges you may face.

LLC Perks: More Than Meets the Eye

While the above advantages based on the business structure are enough to cause you to make a move to form an LLC, the benefits don't stop there. LLCs provide other less obvious perks to make your business grow exponentially. Let's explore them.

Shield Your Personal Wealth

Compared to sole proprietorship and partnership, LLCs protect your personal property, like cars, houses, and investment accounts, from being taken by creditors or other parties that win a financial lawsuit. While this benefit is not absolute, structuring your LLC well will protect your personal wealth far more than other unincorporated entities.

Due to these advantages, entrepreneurs can take more business risks without affecting their family's financial safety. Fortunately, you do not run the risk of filing bankruptcy if all fails, like someone in a partnership or doing business on their own.

Your personal wealth also continues to be protected as your company grows because expanding means you take on more risks. As you add more employees, buy larger equipment, add new locations, or hire more commercial vehicles, your personal possessions still remain shielded from growing liability risks.

Tax Efficiencies

The built-in tax advantages of an LLC ensures the company isn't taxed as an entity, but the members report their share of the profit and losses on their individual return. This provision prevents the company from losing money if they had also been taxed as a business.

In addition, LLCs allow you to choose to be taxed as an S-Corporation or a C-corporation because of the tax election flexibility it offers. The option you choose will help you optimize income and deductions allocations and position you to make strategic income splitting and tax plans. The money you save from these tax-efficient methods can be used to expand the product or service line, drive innovation, or enhance skills development.

Cut the Red Tape - Easy Compliance

An appealing advantage of an LLC compared to a corporation is the ease of compliance. LLCs require less paperwork, minimal administrative duties, and manageable legal regulations. You do not need to issue stock certificates, appoint directors, or hold annual shareholder meetings. In addition, it has fewer accounting formalities than fewer states requiring frequent LLC annual franchise tax payments

or annual reporting.

As a start-up, the costs are minimal because you don't have to draft bylaws or issue stock. The legal fees for creating an operating agreement and the filing fees are much less than for corporate formation. If you mainly want to focus on growing your business, an LLC offers the simplicity you need to establish operations.

Gaining the Ability to Raise Capital

LLCs allow you to sell membership interest to investors to fund your startup costs, finance large purchases, or expand operations. You are able to accomplish this without taking on overwhelming debt. You can allow your friends, family members, and outsiders to buy equity stakes in your LLC.

As you add members, you can create various classes of membership having different rights and control the percentage of ownership sold. However, the operating document still governs the profit distribution and rights of new members. The new members still benefit from the pass-through taxation, unlike S Corporations, where the limit is 100 shareholders. This feature enables LLCs to raise significant capital as they retain tax efficiencies and structure flexibility.

The Anatomy of an LLC

LLCs have some crucial components and movable parts that ensure you have meaningful power and flexibility to change things. Being familiar with the primary parts, such as operating agreements, the role of manager and members, and taxation options, helps to demystify LLCs for a beginner. This knowledge ensures your business is positioned for success and adheres to all legal measures. Let's break down the key

components to ensure you understand the various parts.

Who's Who: Members & Ownership

Members in an LLC own the company, and membership is not limited

to a specific number. Anyone can become a member of an LLC. An individual, partnerships, corporations, trusts, and other LLCs are welcome to join. When these entities join, you create a corporation-like structure with shared risks and investments.

To receive ownership interest, members contribute capital, which is reflected as percentage charges, membership units, or stock analogs. Each member's ownership stake determines their voting rights, profit share, losses, and distribution.

Membership interests can be transferred freely among members or to outsiders. However, they must receive consent from the rest and follow the guidelines in the operating document. You can sell, gift, or pass it on as an inheritance.

Further, LLCs offer reasonable flexibility in structuring ownership, profit-sharing, or investments. Members can also choose to actively manage the LLC or choose managers to oversee day-to-day operations.

Leading the Way: Flexible Management

LLCs offer flexibility in the managerial structure to permit member-managed or manager-managed structures. Small LLCs work well with member-managed structures as they can efficiently perform the day-to-day responsibilities. Decisions require majority approval or a consensus to be accepted and implemented.

Larger LLCs function better by appointing experienced managers to make decisions on behalf of everyone. The manager you hire can be a non-member or a member. Choosing a non-member enables you to hire someone with expertise instead of settling for a member with lower qualifications and experience.

The law also allows LLCs to combine the member and manager-

managed structure. For instance, you can hire a general manager to monitor the daily operations but have members retain the authority to make sensitive decisions like large expenditures. The operating agreement acts as a guard to ensure the managerial structure works well by outlining rules regarding electing and removing managers, powers and roles, decision-making processes, and voting procedures. These guidelines prevent confusion and conflicts as the LLC grows.

The Rulebook: Your Operating Agreement

As mentioned above, the LLC operating agreement serves as a governing document and instructional manual for the business [2]. It goes into detail to explain the following:

- Voting procedures

- Member rights

- Profit allocations

- Capital contribution

- Manager roles

- Membership transfer

- Dissolution terms

Other details you must include in the document are who can take on debt, enter contracts, sign checks, and purchase assets. Although your state does not require a legal document, having it enables you to align your goals with the rules, provide directions, and avoid conflict between members.

If you do not create this document, the state laws come into effect if you have a dispute and need the court's intervention. The risk you attract in this situation is incomparable to the time and resources you would have used to draft a favorable operating document.

Choose Your Tax Preference

By default, LLCs are taxed as sole proprietorships or partnerships because profits flow through to members' personal tax returns. You can also elect to be a corporation, file with the IRS and choose between an S Corporation (S Corp) or a C Corporation (C Corp).

Choosing S Corp status passes through income and deductions to individual returns while still enjoying corporate benefits. Opting for C Corp means your LLC will incur double taxation but allows your company to retain earnings at lower tax rates and deduct employee benefits.

An LLCs tax planning flexibility can help to simplify the tax planning process. You can adapt as your business grows or faces challenging times. For example, when you begin a business, the profits are crucial for growth, so pass-through taxation is the ideal option. As your business grows, corporate taxation might become appealing as your financial strategies change.

Prestige Points

Doing Business As (DBA) often limits your client, partners, investor,

and lender reach. An LLC structure carries more prestige and credibility because it shows you have done your research and are serious about your future business plans.

Customers and lenders feel more comfortable conducting business and signing contracts with an established company than with an unknown DBA name. Besides, suppliers extend better terms to LLCs over sole proprietorships and partnerships.

Having an LLC next to your company name is like having a badge of honor. When investors or clients see those three letters, they know you are committed to high standards. This impression will increase your trustworthiness—an invaluable quality in the business world. Your LLC will attract more opportunities and grant you access to unimaginable possibilities.

Why Legal Structure Isn't Just Red Tape

As you form the LLC, you may feel like the paperwork is just for legal formalities and doesn't benefit the business to a large extent. However, the content in the paperwork serves additional purposes that go beyond red tape. For instance, the information in the documents protects your assets, boosts credibility, informs your business decisions, and enhances funding potential. It is not about fulfilling an obligation but positioning your company for growth from the first day. Still not convinced? Here are four other reasons why it's more than just formalities.

Dodging Legal Pitfalls

Imagine a situation where a creditor or client sues and wins the lawsuit. If you did not form an LLC and acquired all the paperwork, your personal possessions are at risk of being taken by the plaintiff. The courts can authorize them to access your bank account for the funds, take your house or car, or sell your property or investment to get the money awarded. An LLC enables you to dodge such outcomes because the claims and lawsuits against your business can only affect your company's assets and insurance coverage.

When your business is an LLC, it discourages people from filing superficial lawsuits. Instead, they are likelier to target sole proprietorships with substantial wealth who have not shielded themselves from liability. This benefit doesn't mean you won't face business risks and disputes but that you will be prepared to safeguard your and your family's interests.

The Compliance Code

As you conduct business, you often interact with the term compliance, which mainly targets how you keep your records. Although the rules are less strict than corporations, you still need to keep records for:

- Company meetings

- Operational decisions

- Member votes

- Manager appointments

In addition, your business financial records should be completely separate from your personal finances. Have different accounts for business and personal transactions. At the end or beginning of every financial year, ensure you submit annual reports and fees to your state. These compliance requirements prevent occurrences of people taking money from LLCs for personal use. If the state and court find that you have not upheld the various codes, you risk losing your LLC status and incurring additional losses from lawsuits, penalties, or fines.

Deal or No Deal: Business Transactions

Establishing yourself as an LLC attracts more business deals and purchases. Many credible vendors also sell to registered companies because they want the assurance that you have taken the legal measures to do business. Further, lenders approve sizable lines of credit or loans to companies with a functional business structure.

If you plan to make big purchases, doing business without an LLC status may fail to get you the deal. The LLC legal structure offers the seller confidence because it lays out a remedy plan in case of non-payment. Besides, customers and partners prefer getting into contracts with registered companies rather than an individual. LLC gives a sense of safety because you can handle the matter with other members if the original individual leaves the company or disappears.

Magnetize Investors & Partners

The superior quality LLCs offer the original owners is the ability to create shareable equity through membership interests. This feature enables you to attract outside investors more easily than a partnership or sole proprietorship. You can allow investors to buy into your business without the need for strenuous paperwork like that of a corporation.

Co-ownership in an LLC is also more attractive to potential partners because you can run the business with equal rights as a partnership structure but with the LLC benefits. In addition, members can pass their share as inheritance, so investors considering joining don't have to worry about their money being tied up.

Committed and long-term investors often like to join companies that show they have done their homework and planned well. Having the LLC title in your business name makes you a good fit. They also have confidence that your business is there to stay and you are making plans for the future.

As we come to the end of chapter one, you have probably understood that forming an LLC is not only about checking a legal box, but it places you in a strategic position to excel. Although you will put in the work, an LLC is worth the effort as your business grows. In chapter two, we will take you through the planning process and the preparation needed for launching. The information you'll learn will ensure your business starts at an advantageous point and will likely build significant momentum from day one.

The Exact Step-by-Step Guide to Starting Your LLC

Before we get into chapter two, we wanted to quickly lay out the exact LLC set-up process. We'll go more in-depth on these throughout the rest of the book, but this way, you have it here in one place, so you can simply run right through it when setting up your LLC.

Kicking off the process of setting up your LLC is a big deal. It's the first step toward giving your business a solid base. But the admin side of things isn't exactly thrilling for most folks. Still, getting a handle on all the paperwork, legal bits, and financial details is needed.

This next section is about laying down the tracks for your business to run smoothly. So, let's walk through this together, step by step.

Choosing Your LLC's Name & State

Let's talk about picking a name for your LLC. This part's more fun than you might think, but there are a few rules to play by. First up, your LLC's name has to be one of a kind – no stepping on any toes by having a name too similar to another business in your state. And there are a few no-nos to avoid, like using words that might confuse your LLC with a government agency.

So, how do you make sure your LLC's name is ok? Start by brainstorming a list that captures the vibe of your business. Once you've got some contenders, check them against your state's business database – usually something you can do online. Sometimes, you can reserve a name until you're ready to register your LLC officially, which might give you some time while you make a final decision.

Then, as far as choosing a state to incorporate in, here's what you should consider:

- **The location of business operations:** If your business operates in a specific state, it could be beneficial to incorporate there, as it can simplify registration, taxation, and compliance requirements.

- **Taxation:** Different states have different tax structures, including some income taxes, franchise taxes, and sales taxes. Research the tax rates and conditions in different states to determine which is most favorable for your business.

- **Costs and fees:** The fees associated with setting up and maintaining your LLC can vary significantly from state to state. For example, Wyoming, Delaware, New Mexico, Montana, and Colorado have some of the lowest fees.

- **Accessibility to courts:** Does your business anticipate legal disputes? If so, consider the efficiency of the state's court system in handling business-related cases.

- **Legal and regulatory environment:** Each state has its own legal and regulations governing businesses, including employment laws, licensing requirements, and environmental regulations.

Filing the Articles of Organization

Next on the list is tackling the Articles of Organization. Think of this as the official certificate for your LLC. It's where you lay down the basics of your business for the state to see.

First thing's first, you'll need to gather some essential info: the name of your LLC, the address where your business will sit, and the details of your registered agent (that's the person or service authorized to receive legal papers on behalf of your LLC). Some states might ask for a bit more, like the purpose of your business or who's in charge.

Now, onto the common slip-ups. The big one is messing up your registered agent's details. If they're wrong, you might miss important legal notices. Also, double-check that business name to make sure it's exactly the same as the one you reserved. Mismatched names can send your paperwork to rejection.

When your Articles are polished and ready, you'll submit them to the state, usually the Secretary of State's office, and pay a filing fee. This can be done online in most places. And just like that, you're on your way to making your business official. Keep everything accurate, follow the steps, and your LLC will be set up for success.

Appointing a Registered Agent

When choosing a registered agent for your LLC, make sure this person or company is your official go-to for any legal documents. They must be ready and available during business hours to ensure you don't miss anything important.

Here's the deal: you can nominate an individual (yes, even yourself) or go with a professional service. If you're leaning towards an individual, make sure they're reliable and always around to handle documents promptly. On the other hand, a professional service might cost a bit, but they're pros at keeping your paperwork in order and can offer an extra layer of privacy by having their address public, not yours.

The bottom line? Think about your daily schedule and privacy needs. Whether it's you, a buddy, or a service, your registered agent needs to ensure your LLC stays in good standing and legally compliant.

Obtaining an Employer Identification Number (EIN)

Getting your Employer Identification Number (EIN) is next, and it's like having the keys to your new LLC. It's essential for tax filings and opening a bank account for your business. Lucky for you, getting an EIN is easy and free.

Here's how to do it: Head to the IRS website and look for the EIN application page. It's an online form you can breeze through as long as you've got your LLC info ready. You'll fill in details about your LLC, like where it's located and what it does.

The EIN is how the IRS keeps tabs on your business for tax purposes, so it's an important step. Plus, banks usually ask for your EIN when you're setting up a business bank account. It's also handy for hiring employees when you're ready to do so.

You'll get your EIN instantly once you hit submit on the IRS website. Just like that, your LLC is one step closer to being fully operational.

Drafting an Operating Agreement

Even if your LLC is a one-person show, drafting an Operating Agreement is smart. This is the rulebook for how your business runs. It sets clear expectations and helps avoid headaches down the road, especially if you decide to expand or bring on partners.

What goes into this document? Start with your LLC's name, the members, and how you plan to operate. Detail the ownership percentages if you have business partners. Spell out how profits and losses get divvied up.

Also, consider what happens if someone wants out or if you want to add someone to the team. An Operating Agreement covers these scenarios, giving everyone a clear message for handling changes.

This agreement, even for single-member LLCs, means you have a blueprint for operations and a protective shield for your personal assets.

Business Licenses and Permits

Jumping into business means getting comfortable with a few licenses and permits. The requirements can vary depending on what your LLC does and where it's located. For starters, check with your local city or county government to understand the basics. Then, move on to state-level obligations, which might include special permits depending on your industry. Don't forget federal regulations, especially if your business operates in areas like agriculture, alcohol, or aviation. A good tip is to reach out to your local Small Business Administration (SBA) office or a business advisor for a nudge in the right direction. They can help you sift through the maze of regulations.

Setting Up a Business Bank Account

Next up is getting a business bank account, because keeping your personal and business finances separate is important for clarity and legal protection. Choose your bank, and when you're ready, bring your LLC's EIN, Articles of Organization, and Operating Agreement. These documents prove your business's legitimacy and outline who has the authority to manage the funds. A business bank account simplifies tax reporting and bolsters your LLC's credibility with customers and vendors. Plus, it's a solid step toward managing your cash flow.

Compliance and Annual Requirements

Keeping your LLC in good standing involves more than just setting up shop. You'll need to file an annual report with your state every year, which usually involves a fee and a summary of your business's current status. If you use a website like Rocket Lawyer to start your LLC and use their registered agent services, they can handle the annual report filing on your behalf, for an extra fee.

On top of that, staying on top of tax filings, both federally and at the state level, is non-negotiable. Depending on where you're registered, additional compliance tasks or filings might be required. Consider setting reminders or working with a professional to ensure you don't miss any deadlines. Staying diligent with these annual obligations helps avoid penalties and keeps your business on solid legal ground

The Right Websites to Start Your LLC

If you want an easy way to kick off your LLC without having to deal with all the legal requirements yourself, you can look into one of the top websites for starting an LLC. For example:

- **LegalZoom:** They offer LLC formation services along with a wide range of legal documents and services.

- **Rocket Lawyer:** Rocket Lawyer offers comprehensive legal services, including LLC formation, customizable legal documents, registered agents, and attorney consultations.

- **Incfile:** Incfile is known for its affordable pricing and straightforward LLC formation process. They also provide a free registered agent service for the first year.

Key Takeaways

- LLCs are ideal for small businesses because they provide a partnership tax simplicity and corporation liability protection.

- The pass-through taxation element of an LLC enables new business owners to save money by avoiding double taxation.

- Creating a professional operating document with the critical day-to-day issues of operation and authority is vital to prevent disputes and ensure goal achievement.

- The flexible management options LLCs provide allow the members to customize duties and leadership to their advantage.

- LLC business structure gives entrepreneurs more confidence to take more risks because the business structure protects personal assets.

- Business owners must remain compliant with the LLC requirement to continue enjoying the benefits, or else the court or state might override the status.

- The LLC structure gives you a better standing with potential partners, lenders, and customers as it signifies careful planning and professionalism.

- LLCs allow you to form long-term business relationships by offering continuity options such as membership transfer and inheritance.

Chapter 2

Launching Your LLC with Confidence

"Dream big, start small, but most of all, start.
-Simon Sinek

Crafting a Business that Resonates

Crafting a business that resonates well with customers is about connecting with them at a personal level. You not only want to provide services or sell products, but you also want to create a lasting bond. Relating with your customers at a personal level is the current trend that new businesses use to win loyalty. In the next section, you will learn how to target your potential customers, choose the right idea, analyze the changing industry patterns, and strategize using the SWOT analysis.

Need-Spotting: Target Market Insights

Understanding your potential customers necessitates knowing your target market and internalizing their needs. It also requires you to conduct in-depth market research that will help you discover the following:

- **Psychometrics:** Your customers' thoughts and emotions influence the goods or services they buy.

- **Pain points:** What your customer misses that is making them experience pain or difficulty.

- **Unmet needs:** The desires your potential customers need to be fulfilled.

- **Demographics:** The people you want to reach, where they live, and what's special about them.

You can implement various methods to conduct an in-depth survey, such as user interviews and online or in-person surveys. Focus groups also work because they help you get the opinion, attitude, and perception of a product or service.

Whichever approach you use, ensure you ask about their frustrations, ideal solutions, challenges, and their typical day surrounding the product or service you want to offer. These questions aim to get an implicit and explicit understanding of their needs.

When gathering the demographic data, go beyond the basic information such as age, gender, and race. Ask about their education level, income, geographical location, religious or spiritual practice, and family size. Anything that will help you focus on the needs related to your service or product. This approach will assist you in learning where existing solutions have failed to address or meet your prospective customers' needs and desires.

Is Your Idea Gold? Evaluating Business Viability

You might be excited that your idea will solve your potential customer's problems. But before running with that idea in your mind, you must evaluate it to determine if it has the potential to foster growth and if it is capable of keeping the momentum long-term. Ask yourself questions such as, how much reach does your idea plan to have? Are the customers you are targeting enough to keep the demand high? Will the idea promote short and long-term growth for your LLC?

A major aspect you need to evaluate is the competition—both direct and indirect competitors. Questions to have in mind are:

- How many businesses are already offering relatively the same services or products?

- Have you thought of a way to differentiate your brand from theirs?

- How much are they charging for their services and products?

As you answer these questions, you will be able to tell if you should proceed with your idea or modify it to suit the gaps you discover. Keep in mind - you don't need to reinvent the wheel here. You can build a successful business by mirroring what other successful businesses have already done. After all, they've proven there's a market for it. Just make sure to put your own spin on it.

Next, you must assess your readiness to meet the regulatory and financial requirements to start your business. Do you have enough money to actualize your idea? Will you have difficulty getting certified or acquiring the necessary licenses and permits? Do you need partners or co-founders to help you add the qualifications and skills you need to form and operate a business?

Additionally, consider your strengths and weaknesses and your passion for business. Will you persevere through the entire process of opening and running a business? Take the time to reflect and honestly answer this question.

Analyzing Industry Trends and Shifts

Staying ahead in your industry is all about learning and tracing the changes occurring in the market and adjusting your business plan. As you keep track of shifting trends, you'll spot threats and notice emerging opportunities. Some factors affecting industry changes include the following:

- Evolving cultural trends that impact the attitudes of your customers. Investigate what caused the shift and make changes where necessary.

- The current movement of people in your business's locality. Are more people moving in or out of your area? If you're losing customers due to a decline in your target market, research new ways to remain relevant.

- Pay close attention to the target demographic in your area. Changes can impact the future of your business. Once you identify these trends, plan accordingly.

- One age group is moving to another stage in life. Your product or service may lose relevance if you do not adjust or modify the product. For example, baby boomers are retiring, and Gen Zers are getting married or having children.

- Understand the technological changes affecting businesses, especially the emergence of AI. Some entrepreneurs are losing revenue, while others are celebrating the creation of new business opportunities.

After studying the above changes, adjust your services and products to meet the current demand and remain relevant.

SWOT: The Full Picture

SWOT analysis helps you get a holistic picture of how your business will perform in relation to particular internal and external factors. The internal factors focus on your strengths and weaknesses, while the external factors assess the opportunities and threats in your business environment. Creating a strategic plan around these four elements will help you base your company's decisions on facts. The following table summarizes the areas each letter in SWOT evaluates and the examples involved.

SWOT Analysis	Evaluates	Examples
Strengths	Advantages you have that make your business stand out	- Skilled team members - High capital - Unique brand - Low debt - Tax advantages
Weaknesses	Aspects that put your business at risk of performing poorly	- High costs - Poor market research done - Fewer assets - Lack of specialized skills - Poor credit score

Opportunities	External factors to take advantage of to grow your business	- Partnerships - Increasing population - Better technology advances - Less stringent regulatory demands
Threats	Outside forces that can hinder your business from thriving	-New advanced products - Dishonest competition -Negative economic shift -Unfavorable regulations

SWOT analysis is a comprehensive model that requires a team to help you analyze everything objectively and with precision. Recruit partners, LLC members, trusted customers, and professionals to help you succeed in coming up with a practical SWOT report.

Afterward, address those factors that are significant or present the greatest risk of losing revenue. For example, if one of your weaknesses is a lack of specialized skill, you can employ someone to fill that role or investigate how technology (as an emerging opportunity) can cover that weakness.

Dive Before You Launch

It is exciting to see your dream becoming a reality. Launching a business is a big step you are about to undertake, but you first need to do your homework. Diving before you launch necessitates thoroughly researching the market to ensure you target the right people. It also requires you to study your competition and set the right price. Let's expound more on these points.

Segmentation: Who's Your Crowd?

Finding your crowd entails knowing who you are targeting with your product. It's about narrowing down the specific people who will need or want to buy what you are offering [3]. Are you planning to sell your product or services to 40-year-olds or 20-year-olds or a mixed-age group? Which income bracket are they in? What lifestyle habits do they have? These questions will inform how you package and advertise your services or products.

For most businesses, their product or service does not meet everyone's needs. Your business is going to solve a problem or satisfy a need for a segment of the market. For example, a business owner may have formulated a new hair product similar to those in the market but has a unique quality because it is organic and environmentally friendly. This entrepreneur will ensure the packaging style is environmentally conscious and leans towards a minimalist design.

To choose the most favorable crowd, you must conduct thorough research in the locality you want to set up shop. Afterward, you will direct your resources and use your energy to satisfy the needs of the segment that most suit your product or service. Expanding your reach by watering down your offering may cause you to lose revenue. At the beginning, choose one segment and take a risk with them. As your business grows, you can add another segment as you open new locations or add more departments.

Friends & Foes: The Competitive Landscape

Before launching your business, you must analyze your competitive landscape by studying the existing companies. Your aim is to learn how they conduct their business. Examples of crucial areas to focus on include:

- Products and services

- Packaging methods

- Marketing strategies

- Online presence

- Unique selling point

The information you collect as you assess the above variables will help to reveal the gaps present, and hopefully, you can fill them. In your data collection process, you will notice two types of competitors: direct and indirect. For instance, if you plan to establish a vegetarian restaurant, your direct competitors would be the other vegetarian stores. In contrast, your indirect competitors would include the retail shop selling raw veggies. In formulating your business strategy, identify the measures you will take to tackle the two groups of competitors.

Finally, find out the potential barriers to opening a business in that area. Will the competitors fight you? What plans are in place to mitigate risks associated with rival companies? How you address this situation depends on whether you'll have an e-commerce store or only a retail shop.

Reading Minds: Deciphering Customer Behavior

Knowing your customers' behavior entails understanding what they like and dislike, how they buy, and why they prefer particular products over others in the market. These findings will help you in assessing how your prospective consumers purchase things. Today's marketing approach is not about who will buy what you are selling but how and why your potential customers are shopping for that particular product or service.

Ask yourself, how frequently do the people you are targeting shop? Why do certain products sell better than others? How effective is your marketing? Businesses learn a lot by paying attention to three key variables they use in understanding consumer behavior. These are:

- **Personality traits:** Are these customers extroverts or introverted? What is their background? How were they brought up?

- **Social traits:** Are your potential customers susceptible to external factors like advertisements, peers, and news?

- **Psychological responses:** How do customers feel about your services or products? Are their reactions based on their personality traits, or are they situational? What steps can your business take to improve how customers feel about your services? Answering these questions can give you key insights into ways to adapt strategies to improve.

Understanding the above factors is crucial to establishing a solid foundation for your business. Discover what makes them happy, sad, or angry. Use such knowledge to solve their problems.

Pricing Mastery: Setting it Right

Setting the price right requires you to gather information on how your competitors have priced their product or service, your cost of production, the discount you want to offer as a start-up, and your desired profit margins. You will use one or a combination of these factors to set your price. The following are examples of variations for setting the price:

- Set your price above the cost of production but at a cost your customers are willing to pay (value-based pricing).

- Focus on your profit margins so you factor in the cost of production and the profit you plan to make (cost-plus pricing).

- Work with your competitor's prices and charge the same price, slightly below or above their price (competitive pricing).

- Focus on getting into the market and attracting customers using a price that is not your ideal but will increase after you get loyal customers (penetration pricing).

- Set the price as per your customers' location (geographical pricing).

- Set the price in relation to a customer's emotions or subconscious mindset. For example, setting the price at $19.99 instead of $20 (psychological pricing).

Realistically, if you sell numerous products or services, you will eventually use a customized combination of the above pricing strategies. As you come up with the price, monitor your customers' responses and adjust accordingly. Ensure your marketing strategy includes an in-depth explanation of the value your product or service provides—you want your customer to feel they got value for their money.

Naming Your LLC: More than Just Words

Naming your LLC is an important decision you should make with exceptional care. It has to be a unique name, though it should let your prospective customers know which brand of products and services you offer. There are laws and regulations applicable to your state and industry, which we'll discuss in more detail below. This section discusses more about the factors you should bear in mind while naming your LLC.

Branding: Beyond the Logo

Branding your LLC is more than just creating an engaging logo. Indeed, the logo must convey to your customers exactly what your business stands for and reveal your personality. But branding goes beyond that. Branding is the essence of your reputation and how you want your LLC to be viewed. Branding also affects how your customers feel and think when interacting with your company.

As you develop your brand, find a professional or trusted partner who can help you analyze what you have in store for your customers and how it is better and different from what the competitors have been offering them.

Defining your mission is the first step in developing a unique brand. This step entails identifying why you are going into business, what motivates you, and the values you want the customers to experience. Reflecting on these issues will help to clarify why you're becoming an entrepreneur and provide you with an accurate mission statement.

Choosing the right brand also means figuring out what makes you and your business unique. You are selling your story, personality, character, background, and other unique factors. So, consider what makes your offering different from that of other sellers in the market.

Digital Real Estate: Domain Checks

After choosing a suitable name for your business, you need to check online whether the name is already registered. Sometimes, people in digital real estate register various domain names and then sell them to entrepreneurs. Domain pricing depends on how hard they worked to get a noticeable presence online.

Follow these steps to check the availability of the domain you have in mind if buying an existing digital domain is not part of your plan:

- Visit any domain registrar such as GoDaddy, Namecheap, or Bluehost and search for your business name. If the name is already taken, these platforms will help generate suggestions specific to your business name.

- Use a domain search tool that is dedicated to that purpose. Examples include DomainWheel, Business Name Generator, and Domains Bot. These tools will confirm if the name is available or suggest names you can use once you enter your business name.

- Perform a simple web search by typing in the domain name you want to use and clicking search. If a website is already online, you must abandon that domain name and look for variations. If the search results show "this site can't be reached," you probably have a domain name. But you should cross-check several times to ensure it wasn't an internet or website glitch.

Once you find an available domain, quickly reserve it because someone else could have the same idea.

Legally Yours: Trademark Navigations

A trademark is another way to distinguish yourself from your competitors and for customers to recognize you. Its main function is to legally protect your brand, assist you in safeguarding your product or service against fraud or counterfeiting, and identify the source of your service and goods.

You can register your trademark with the state authority in charge of the trademark or with the United States Patent and Trademark Office (USPTO). State registration is easier and less expensive than federal registration. However, it limits your reach. Once you go online, you have a more national and international reach that may pose a challenge to trademark ownership.

Similar to domain checks, you need to conduct an online search before filing an application to register your company's trademark. Searching will avoid closely-related duplication, and the filing fee is non-refundable once USPTO rejects your application due to unavailability. If possible, it is better to trademark your LLC at the beginning rather than using the name, and after building a solid brand, you realize you have to change it because it's in existence.

Stickiness: Crafting Memorable Names

If you want to enhance your brand engagement and have a lasting impact, especially for first-time customers, you must have a memorable name that sticks with your clients. A sticky name grabs the customers' attention, establishes a connection, and leaves a lasting impression.

To choose a memorable business name, make sure it evokes emotions. Examples include joy, empathy, trust, intrigue, and curiosity. Also, pick a simple name that still states what you are all about. Short and easy-to-pronounce names are memorable. However, a long and complicated name will confuse people and may even scare away potential clients.

Further, it is important to use known terms, expressions, and signs while naming a product or company. People tend to relate more to what they know, and they go for concepts that are recognizable rather than unpacking new ones. Secondly, you will command greater confidence and trust within a short time.

Legal Foundations: Beyond the Basics

After internalizing the basic requirements for starting a business discussed so far, it is time to go deeper by looking at the legal side of things. At the onset, it may sound like a complex process, but we endeavor to simplify the content to help you understand. We will discuss the regulations and compliance needs, the permits and licenses you must acquire, and how your business location matters.

Rules of the Land: Navigating Regulations

Every business must follow the rules of the land, which are created by the local authorities, state officials, and the federal government. Take time to study the regulations at each level and categorize them according to must-haves and those good to have. A key responsibility that comes with the LLC name is ensuring you abide by the regulations at all levels.

Without a doubt, keeping up with the regulations can be overwhelming and act as an obstacle for you to get started. However, you must take the bull by the horns and address them to ensure you stay in business. To get started, here are some ways to navigate the regulatory process:

- Learn about the regulations and update your information through ongoing research, subscribing to reliable industry newsletters, and visiting the regulatory websites monthly or quarterly.

- Form a team of trusted individuals who can help you create a system geared towards staying compliant. They can help you develop the policies, procedures, and protocols needed to ease adherence monitoring.

- Embrace technology and use it to streamline tasks, documents, and activities to ensure they meet local, state, and federal regulatory standards.

- Ask for guidance from experts in various fields related to regulatory requirements. For example, consult a corporate lawyer to help ensure your documents meet the standards or talk to an accountant to confirm your records have all the required information.

As you interact with the various regulatory stakeholders, make it your mission to form a working relationship beyond inspection. Seek to win them over to your side and show them your intention of creating value for everyone's benefit, including them.

Staying Compliant in Your Industry

Once you know the regulations specific to your business, you must prioritize staying compliant. A foundational step is complying with the LLC business structure, such as creating the proper documents, meeting the membership requirements, holding the required meetings, and sending reports before deadlines [4].

After meeting the general compliance requirements, you should focus on the more specific requirements for your business. For example, if you are opening a business that requires storing people's sensitive information, you must know the US data privacy protection laws that mandate you to protect your customers' information. Staying compliant attracts the following benefits:

- Covers your business against legal actions that could have been avoided. Non-compliance opens a loophole that customers, other companies, or authorities can exploit. You may end up paying huge settlement fees that are incomparable with the cost you would have incurred staying compliant.

- Safeguards your business from losing customers because they cannot trust your product or services after you violate a law. For example, if you own a restaurant and authorities discover that your employees do not receive any training in food handling.

- Saves you money by avoiding huge fines for ignoring compliance regulations. Your business license may be revoked or suspended for an extended period.

- Ensures business continuity when you maintain compliance. For instance, if you miss one crucial LLC requirement, you risk losing the name and the benefits that ensure long-term success.

It is important to note that business laws and regulations do not remain constant. They keep changing, and this requires you to stay vigilant. Compliance is an ongoing process. Make it your goal to stay current with the external and internal business compliance requirements.

An Updated Reporting Requirement for 2024 and Beyond

Starting in 2024, LLCs and Corporations must file a Beneficial Owner Information Report (BOI). Reports started being accepted in January of 2024, and if you registered your LLC prior to January 1, 2024, you will have until January 1, 2025, to report the BOI. If your company registered on or after January 1, 2024, you will have 30 days of notice of creation or registration.

You can learn more and file your report here:

https://www.fincen.gov/boi

Getting the Green Light: Licenses & Permits

Acquiring licenses and permits is a crucial step that gives you the green light to open your doors for business. Licenses and permits have a general purpose, although their definitions differ. A license grants an individual or business permission to do something. It is used to guarantee competence in what you want to do.

Permits, on the other hand, monitor safety issues and seek to ensure you prioritize the customer's well-being. For example, you need a health permit to open a restaurant or clinic. These licenses and permits are issued by the federal, state, county, municipal, and city governments.

The following table gives examples of licenses and permits you may need to operate a business.

License and permit requirements	Concerned institution	Examples of business
Starting a business	Federal and state	Any venture that will sell products or offer services
Business activities regulated nationally	Federal government	Alcohol, agriculture, and food preparation
Legal structure	State government	Corporations, NGOs, LLCs, or partnerships
Employment Identification Number	Federal government	Any business with employees
Zoning permit	Local government	Operate a business in a particular location
Health permit	County health department	Handle food or in contact with the human body
Sales tax license	State government	Sell goods or services

Location Matters: Zoning Know-hows

When contemplating a business location, you need to look for things

like zoning laws, how much in tax you will be paying, customers' proximity, and the regulatory requirements of operating within that area. The choice of location must also take into consideration the nature of the product or service that you sell. In addition, keep in mind the expenses that will go into choosing a specific location. Factors to consider that change according to location include:

- Rental rates

- Utilities

- Property value

- Business insurance rate

- Minimum wages

- Government fees and licenses

When searching for a rental space for your business, look into the area's zoning laws. For instance, some local authorities prohibit business owners from operating their businesses within residential or restricted zones. Additionally, the zone you choose should match your budget and meet your business standards. For example, if you intend to provide premium services, a luxurious and quiet site would work better than a strip mall-type location in a noisy area.

Another factor to consider in zoning matters is the tax landscape. Sales tax, income tax, corporate tax, and property tax differ from place to place. Look for a state or county that creates a tax-friendly environment for certain companies. Besides, some states or local governments also give special tax credits, favorable loans, and other financial incentives to support new businesses. So, think through these factors before you settle on a location.

Blueprint of a Bulletproof Business Plan

Starting a business without knowing exactly what you will be offering customers or how you will execute various roles and responsibilities is a recipe for disaster. Your business may grow fast, but you lack a plan to take advantage of this opportunity and lose customers or experience burnout.

Conversely, your business may lag, and you lose revenue because you have no reference point on what action to take. A bulletproof business plan takes care of either outcome. It helps you have a contingency plan and know how to respond to emerging challenges. What should you include in a business plan? Let's answer that question for you.

Purpose-Driven: Crafting Mission & Vision

Crafting a mission or vision statement requires deep thought. It should

capture what your business will be about and also tell your customers where you want to go. Even though you aren't fully clear on the direction you want your business to take in the future, make sure the mission and vision statements capture your values.

Ideally, you should create your vision statement first because it carries the overall big idea. Afterward, craft your mission statement, which involves developing a practical and step-focused statement that informs the LLC members and the public how you plan to achieve the vision. Questions you should ask yourself as you draft your vision are:

- What purpose do I want my vision to serve?

- Why do I want my business to exist?

- What core values do I want to have for my business?

- What would my customers miss if my business closed down?

As you create your vision, make it relatable and let people feel they are not only buying a product or using your services but also joining a movement or culture that inspires them. A vision statement often remains the same for an extended period, but the mission statement may change as your business grows and you become clear on what you want to focus on.

Captivating Customers: Sales & Marketing Mastery

As you start your business, you want to find ways of attracting potential customers to purchase your services or products. At this stage, you must understand your target customers and design your sales and marketing strategies with that in mind. For example, college students prefer colorful, modern advertising styles that appeal to their emotions. People in their 40s and above prefer an advertisement focusing on how the product will work for them rather than how it will make them feel.

Mastering sales and marketing strategy means creating an experience that will captivate your customers until they become loyal to you. It also involves maintaining or improving the standards you set from the beginning. Compromising your products or services to make more revenue after you get customers is likely to affect sales in the long run. Examples of marketing activities include:

- Relationship building

- Having a social media presence

- Advertising

- Merchandising

- Publicity

Captivating your customers is an ongoing task. You must be willing to change your strategies as you study the market and your customer's behavior. Aim to impress them by satisfying their needs and wants as you also acquire and attract new customers with your unique selling point.

Numbers Don't Lie: Budgets & Projections

The most important aspect that will help to tell if your business is making profits or losses is a well-crafted budget. Keeping an updated and factual budget will help you increase opportunities for investors and loans while reducing your need to acquire debt.

Making projections is also made possible when you keep an accurate budget. It enables you to review your previous data and project the revenue you might make in the next few months. Although, you may need to adjust your projections as the economy or landscape changes.

The main components of a basic business budget are the sales and revenue, total costs and expenses, and the profit or loss section. However, to make projections, you need three crucial reports that you should keep.

- **Cash flow statement:** Monitors how things flow in and out of the business. It includes cash and non-cash items.

- **Income statement:** Gives an overview of a business's net income, expenses, and revenue.

- **Balance sheet:** General picture of your company's assets and liabilities

Keeping accurate records is a key marker of how your business performs. Even when you are faring well by the number of customers you have, it is the final tally in your budget that tells you if these customers have helped you reach your financial goal. Numbers don't lie, so be vigilant about keeping accurate financial records.

Setting the Bar: Milestones & KPIs

Setting the bar high for your business requires you to track whether it is achieving its goals or not. Although there are several ways of monitoring progress, Key Performance Indicators (KPIs) and Milestones are the most commonly used, especially for new and emerging businesses.

KPI measures how well your business achieves its goals in various departments. For example, the marketing team will monitor their performance by the number of new customers or people reached by their strategies. The sales team will measure their performance by comparing data on previous and current sales records. KPI helps track if you are meeting your objectives and lets you see potential risks and new opportunities.

Milestones are used to measure one major event as opposed to KPIs that monitor ongoing progress. Milestones bring together the KPIs at the end of a certain period and assist you in checking if you are closer to achieving your big goal. For example, you may have a milestone of winning 100 loyal customers in the first three months.

KPI keeps track of what you are doing to achieve this goal, while the milestone confirms if you will accomplish this goal in three months. Established companies use milestones to reward employees and celebrate achievements as a way to motivate everyone to keep putting more effort into achieving the business goals.

Key Takeaways

- Analyzing industry shifts entails keeping up with the trends and changes that take place in your area of business.

- Thoroughly researching the market is a critical task to ensure you target the right people. You must also narrow down to the specific people who will need or want to buy what you are offering.

- Branding determines how people feel, think, and say about your business. Think deeply about your values, your reason for starting the business, and your unique selling points.

- Checking for digital presence is part of a name search. Choose a business name that also has a domain name available.

- Take time to study the regulations and compliance requirements at each level and categorize them according to must-haves and those good to have.

- The location you choose for your business must suit the product and service you want to offer. It should also limit your expenses and increase your customer reach.

- Create a vision and mission statement that is relatable and makes people feel they are not only buying a product or using your services but also joining a movement or culture that inspires them.

- Mastering sales and marketing strategy means creating an experience that will captivate your customers until they become loyal to you.

By the way - if you want to get your LLC up and running ASAP, get our free PDF on The 7 Best Websites to Start Your LLC. Just visit **www.LLCLegend.com.**

Chapter 3

Mastering Your LLC Formation

> "If you don't build your dream, someone else will hire you to help
> them build theirs.
> **-Dhirubhai Ambani**

Picking the Perfect State for Registration

The state you choose to register your LLC will determine your company's viability and success. It is the place you'll house your business and generate revenue. Let's consider other important factors as you settle down on the location.

Weighing the State Factors: Tax, Rules, and Anonymity

Taxes, rules, and anonymity are three factors that most entrepreneurs consider before choosing the state to register their LLC. For instance, corporate taxes differ by state because of the different deductions and exclusions. For example, Alabama's corporate tax is 6.5%, Colorado's is 4.5%, and Massachusetts's is 8%.

Every state also has its own rules and regulations for LLCs. Variation occurs in the finer details, such as:

- The amount required as capital

- How often the reporting should be done

- The laws and regulations governing the formation and operation

- Who can be your registered agent

Some states, such as Wyoming, Delaware, Nevada, and New Mexico, don't reveal the details of the manager, members, and even owners. Other states have this provision but with limitations.

Why Everyone Talks About Delaware (And Other Options)

Did you know that more than half of Fortune 500 companies are incorporated in Delaware? They chose this state because Delaware offers significant flexibility and advantages for LLCs. For example, Delaware's privacy laws are stronger, meaning you are not required to reveal too many details about your LLC. In addition, Delaware offers attractive tax benefits; for example, the state doesn't require you to pay income tax if your business is in another state.

Nevada, Wyoming, New Mexico, Iowa, North Dakota, and Tennessee are other states to consider forming an LLC. Each state has one or more benefits that make it stand out. For example, Wyoming and Kentucky are among the cheapest states to form an LLC, while Nevada has favorable features for a single-member LLC.

Going Big: Multi-State Operations and Foreign Qualifications

As your business grows, you may consider extending to other states outside the state where you registered your LLC. The process to make this request is called foreign qualification or state registration. The language can seem confusing, but "foreign" refers to any state outside the one where the LLC is initially registered [5]. Once you qualify, you'll receive authority to conduct business in another state as a qualified foreign company.

The procedure follows the same criteria as the initial formation. You need to fill out documents containing information about your company, referred to as an Application for a Certificate of Authority or Application of Registration. Most states require a Certificate of Good Standing or a Certificate of Existence.

The Right Hand of Your LLC: The Registered Agent

A registered agent is an important person in your LLC, and you must choose them carefully. It is a legal requirement to have a registered agent for your LLC in all states. Let's break down their duties, how to pick one, and what to do when you need to update their details.

Decoding the Role of a Registered Agent

A registered agent is considered by your state as the only legal way for the courts, government, and the public to contact your company. Your registered agent's information is usually in the public domain, and anyone can access their contact when they search online or in person. You need a registered agent to fulfill the following functions:

- Provide an official point where the government can contact you regarding compliance or tax matters.

- Receive legal documents from individuals or entities for or against your company.

- Receive notification of important changes at the federal, state, or local level.

As they carry out these roles, you can stay on top of issues because that makes you aware of important deadlines and actions you must address.

Picking the Perfect Agent: What to Look For

If you mainly operate online or have a mobile office, you must take all the measures to ensure you pick the perfect agent. So, what do you look for in a registered agent? Let's explain using a table.

Qualification of an Agent	Reason
Expertise	Must know about LLCs and understand the compliance rules
Availability	Must be reachable every day and during working hours to deliver all documents
Efficient services	Must have technological means and physical capabilities to offer superior services
Wide reach	Must be able to deliver any information or documentation anywhere in the state of your business and beyond

A registered agent should be more than just a person who delivers documents. They should be someone who can also advise you regarding LLC matters and how to respond to some complex information.

Garrett Monroe

Expert Agent or Do-It-Yourself? Making the Choice

The law allows you to list yourself as the registered agent for your company. You can consider becoming your own agent if you want to cut costs and don't plan on moving around regularly. In addition, if you can keep track of all communications, documents, and deadlines and are highly organized to get it done, then being your own agent is a viable option.

Being your own agent also comes with some disadvantages you must consider. For instance, if you are sensitive about security matters, having your personal details like name and physical address in the public domain will not sit well with you. Besides, being an agent also restricts your movement and makes it impossible for you to receive all the documentation if you have multiple locations.

When and How to Update Your Agent Details

Sometimes, you may wish to hire a different registered agent, or your current agent may inform you their contact information has changed. The law requires you to immediately update the contact information via your state's business filing agency. The procedure is simple. You download the form online, fill and upload or email it. Some states require you to mail it.

If you fail to update the information, you will be fined. Your Certificate of Good Standing may also be revoked, or your company dissolved if the state discovers you operated without a valid agent for a prolonged period.

Crafting a Solid Foundation: The Articles of Organization

The Articles of Organization are the documents you need to establish an LLC with the state. It is used to recognize you as a legal entity promising to conduct business by the state laws. All the benefits of an LLC become realized after filing this document and receiving approval from the state.

The Essentials for Your Articles

Every state has different requirements for the Articles of Organization. Some ask for detailed information, while others require basic information only. The general information you'll be asked for in any state is as follows:

- Your LLC's name

- The physical address of the main place of business

- Your agent's name and mailing address

- Effective date of starting operations

The additional information you may need to submit includes detailed information about your members and manager, why you are forming the LLC, and the duration of the company. Most states will require you to provide an annual report with a small fee charged, while others expect you to submit a brief report at no charge.

Navigating the Filing Labyrinth: Fees and Steps

Once you know the requirements needed in the Articles of Organization, the next step is getting it done. You must file the documents with your state's business filing agency under the Secretary of State. The following are the steps you will take:

1. Access the filing document in your state's online platform or enter their offices to acquire a copy.

2. Fill out the articles of organization accurately and file them as advised.

3. Pay the filing and formation fee.

4. Receive the certificate of formation via mail or email.

5. If need be, publish a notice of formation.

Filing fees range from state to state. It can be as high as $275 (Massachusetts) or as low as $40 (Kentucky). Some states, like South Carolina, Mississippi, Missouri, and Arizona, do not charge annual filing fees, while others charge a fee ranging from $7 to $300.

Note: if you use a site like RocketLawyer.com to set up your LLC, they can do the filing for you for a small fee.

Digital vs Snail Mail: Which Route to Choose?

Articles of Organization are crucial documents. You want to choose the best method to file, receive, and store them. Snail mail could be the option most favorable for you because it's more reliable when stored well and gives you a personal touch. Digital filing is cheaper, faster to access and send, and easy to trace. Whichever option you pick, consider the time taken to exchange documents, cost, and security level.

Adapting and Updating: Tweaking the Articles

You rarely need to amend the Articles of Organization if you get it right the first time. However, you may get to a point where you need to change the LLC's name or physical address, financial structure, management, membership, and the registered agent. Once you determine what you need to change, your next step will be to obtain approval from the members, fill out the specific form for changing the document, file the new document with the agency, pay the fees, receive approval, and adjust your company's document.

Drafting the Operating Blueprint: The Easy Guide

Only five states require that you file your operating document. These are:

1. New York

2. Maine

3. Delaware

4. Missouri

5. California

As business owners, we recommend you create one to ensure your company functions optimally and with minimal disputes. Let's have a closer look at this crucial document.

Why Your LLC Can't Go Without an Operating Agreement

Not having an Operating Agreement means the state laws will govern how you conduct your company operations. For example, most state laws stipulate that profit should be divided equally among members. If this is not the plan you had in mind, some members may bear a heavier burden if the capital contribution differs significantly. Also, the operating agreement will minimize and eliminate disputes arising not only about money but also about authority, duties, and record-keeping.

Customize the Agreement

Customization to best suit your business objectives involves creating an operating agreement that clearly stipulates your goals and objectives. It means leaving nothing to chance but outlining all the rules, rights, and duties of the owners, individual members, managers, and the entire group. An operating document allows you to completely separate your personal affairs and business matters to the level that suits you but is done for the greater good of the company.

Delineating the Power: Roles, Rights, and Duties

The operating document you create depends on whether your company is a single or multi-member LLC. A single-member LLC makes it easier to formulate an operating document because you have all the voting rights and a 100% ownership percentage. For the multi-member LLC, the operating agreement must break down issues such as:

- What each member contributed as capital and the rights they receive

- The roles of each member and which criteria will be used to assign duties

- The voting rights of each member and the weight it carries

- Who has the right and power to make crucial decisions

Keeping the Blueprint Fresh: Revisions and Overhauls

Since you and your members created the operating document, you can make changes anytime your company grows, experiences challenges, or evolves. The amendments you make should still reflect your desires, include updated information, and consider the current market needs. To avoid disputes, your initial operating agreement should include a section on how you'll implement the amendment. Do members need to vote for it to be amended, or can the owner decide if and when it should be amended?

Unlocking Business Power with Your EIN

An Employment Identification Number (EIN) is a nine-digit figure the IRS uses to identify taxpayers. Getting the EIN doesn't depend on whether you have employees; every business owner should have one.

Why Every LLC Needs its EIN Badge

An EIN badge is a crucial requirement to operate a business in America. This number enables businesses to file and pay federal tax returns. Besides, you cannot open a business bank account without an EIN. The bank requires your EIN to identify and link your company to your account. Further, the law does not permit you to have employees without an EIN, and you may not receive some business permit or license without producing your EIN.

EIN 101: The Quick Guide to IRS Application

For the reasons stated above, it is impossible to run your business without an EIN. Here is a quick and easy guide to applying and acquiring your LLC:

1. Visit the IRS website [6] and navigate to apply for EIN (under file, then popular navigation bar)

2. You will be required to give your taxpayer identification number

3. Fill out the form in one session (you cannot save it to complete later)

4. Submit the form, and you'll receive your EIN immediately.

5. Download or print your EIN notice for reference or use

Beyond Identification: The EIN's Extended Role

As mentioned, EIN has more roles than just giving your business an identity with federal and state institutions. It also enables you to keep separate records of your personal assets and your matters. This provision ensures you protect your personal possessions from liability. As your company grows, an EIN also facilitates the investment of surplus cash. You can use the EIN to open a brokerage account and buy stocks.

Stay Current: Managing EIN Alterations and Shifts

The EIN rarely changes and will be associated with your company unless a significant change occurs. Examples of changes include moving from a single-member LLC to a multi-member LLC or a single-member LLC wanting to be taxed as S-Corp. If you received an EIN and wish not to use it, you can request the IRS to close the business account. The IRS will suspend the account without penalty, but the EIN will remain.

Key Takeaways

- The state you choose to host your company will determine your taxes, the extent of rules you'll follow, and how anonymous you will be to the general public.

- A registered agent should be more than just someone who

receives and delivers documents; they should also advise you regarding LLC matters.

- You enjoy all the benefits of an LLC after filing your articles of organization and receiving approval from the state.

- Failing to draft an operating agreement for your business means that state laws will govern how you conduct your company's operations.

- Create an operating agreement that clearly stipulates your goals and objectives, leaving nothing to chance but outlining all the rules, rights, and duties of the owners, individual members, managers, and the entire group.

- An EIN enables companies to pay taxes, open bank accounts, apply for loans, and receive business permits and licenses.

Chapter 4

Mastering LLC Management

> "The first rule of management is delegation. Don't try and do everything yourself because you can't."
> **-Anthea Turner**

Unlocking the Power of Member Roles and Responsibilities

Members are individuals or entities with a membership interest in your LLC. These individuals can make or break your business, and care needs to be taken about how you handle them. This section will explore the various roles and responsibilities of an LLC member.

Defining Member Duties: Who Does What?

The duties of members in an LLC depend on whether you choose to have it as a member-managed or manager-managed LLC. In a member-managed LLC, the members take full responsibility for the day-to-day running of the business and make crucial decisions. In a manager-managed LLC, the members actively choose a manager to perform the daily errands but only participate in major decision-making. Generally, the roles of members in an LLC are:

- Creating and maintaining LLC documents

- Ensuring personal and business finances remain separate

- Entering and signing contracts with vendors and lenders

- Acquiring licenses and filing annual reports

- Voting on diverse issues

The duties each member receives depend on the consensus reached in meetings and what is outlined in the operating agreement.

Voting Rights: Making Decisions That Matter

All members of an LLC have the right to vote. The issue at hand and the weight of their vote differs. The manager-managed structure limits the voting power of members. The members often elect managers, and they make the day-to-day decisions. Members come in to vote on major issues, such as adding new members, contemplating dissolution or merger, and amendment of various documents. The member manager structure gives members the right to vote on all matters concerning the business.

Managing Conflicts: The Art of Resolution

Conflicts among members can arise due to the failure of some members to perform or complete tasks, disagreement on leadership methods, work ethic, and personality differences. While all conflicts need to be addressed, some conflicts are too severe and can affect the running of the business [7]. Here are ways to resolve an arising conflict:

1. Have a clear outline of how to address various conflicts in the operating agreement and refer to it.

2. Approach conflict as an opportunity for growth and model that to the members.

3. If possible, involve everyone in developing the resolution formula.

4. Train and model ways to resolve conflict amongst members, such as healthy accommodation, collaboration, and compromise.

Never allow conflict to drag on for days or weeks. Instead, have a system in place that identifies emerging conflict and takes concrete predetermined steps to address issues before they become major issues.

Membership Changes: Adding and Removing Members

Adding or removing members is a major change in an LLC that requires you to amend your formation documents. In most situations, you must inform the IRS and other major institutions of the change. Changing members could mean adjusting your ownership percentage or selling the entire business. The operating document and Articles of Organization should have this provision—allowing a change in membership and, after that, the changes themselves. Some states also require you to inform them before adding or removing members.

Financial Prowess: Navigating LLC Finances

LLC finances are the resources you use to start, grow, and expand your business. These resources include assets, liabilities, income, expenses, and equity. Gaining financial prowess will help your business thrive from the onset. We discuss the most important aspects below.

Banking Brilliance: Your Guide to Business Accounts

An LLC business bank account helps to set up your company's financial presence in the market. The best account for an LLC goes a mile further in providing other services. For example, offering tools to simplify taxes and bookkeeping matters, refund or eliminate common fees, and offer you opportunities to receive money back on some business purchases.

Determine the accounts you need, such as savings, checking, or investment accounts. Remember to ask if they offer free employee debit cards, ATM rebates, or free wire transfers. The number of accounts you open depends on the size of your business and if you want to separate financial operations for easy accountability.

Cash Flow Mastery: Budgeting for Success

Budgeting for success requires you to keep comparing your company's revenue with the expenses incurred in a given period. Budgeting also helps you gauge your company's performance and know which areas need adjusting to maximize revenue. The following table outlines a variety of budgets you should consider having as you start your business.

Type of Budget	Use
Master budget	Financial projection for the entire company
Static budget	Contains planned financial outputs and inputs for various departments
Operating budget	Contains expenses and revenue from day-to-day operations
Cash-flow budget	Shows cash coming in and going out

Financial Tracking: Where Every Penny Goes

Most entrepreneurs struggle to track their expenses because it means taking intentional measures to trace where every penny goes. Technological advancement has simplified tracking your finances and everyday expenses. A business expense tracker helps to monitor your business's spending habits and simplifies record keeping and tax payments. Examples of expense trackers you can use are Expensify, Zoho Expense, Certify, MileIQ, and Concur Travel.

Tax Tactics: Planning and Payment Strategies

At the onset of your business, you may not feel the tax burden. But wait until your business grows. The various taxes, including federal and state income taxes and self-employment taxes, can increase to a frustrating level. Planning for taxes and adopting effective payment strategies can help you save money. Some tax planning and payment strategies include:

- Reduce your adjusted gross income by reducing your salary, signing up for a tax-deferred retirement plan or a health saving plan.

- Instead of increasing your employees' salary, offer fringe or tax-exempt benefits such as medical and dental insurance, child care assistance, transportation, and employee meals.

- Utilize carryover deductions such as capital losses, home office deductions, net operating losses, and charitable contributions.

- Postpone taxable income to future years. However, you may want to prepay important expenses before the year ends.

Staying ahead of your tax responsibilities also involves knowing the current small business tax laws and how they affect your business. Consulting a tax planner can also save you money and endless stress.

Documenting Your Journey: Records and Documentation

Every LLC must keep accurate records and documents from the onset. Documents such as the Articles of Organization and operating documents help the business have a reference point for its overall running needs. Other records and documents such as business licenses, meeting minutes, accounting books, tax registration, and membership certificates ensure you capture the finer details. Let's explore what you need to know about the paperwork.

The Gold Standard: Accurate Record-Keeping

Accurate record-keeping safeguards you against creditors and lawsuits that may try to exploit an area requiring record-keeping. Besides, an LLC's ability to offer limited liability also depends on keeping proper and factual records. You have no option but to find out your state's requirement for record-keeping and adhere to it. Examples of records you need to keep accurately and track include:

- Updated Articles of Organization

- All meeting minutes

- Amendments filed in your state

- Annual reports

- Names and addresses of managers and members

- Financial and accounting records

Consider using professionals from various fields to ensure you have accurate legal records that can stand in court or help you track your company's growth.

Organizing Chaos: Your Financial Records

Of all the records and documents you have to keep, financial records are the ones that change the most. So, it is not uncommon to find your financial records are disorganized. Here are ways to ensure you organize the chaos you may find yourself in:

1. Create a list of all the accounts you need to keep in a single folder

2. Create a system that tracks all income and expenses

3. Compare your office records to your bank statements

4. Have a plan on how you'll record depreciating assets

5. Hire someone to prepare and maintain all financial statements

The most efficient way to organize and keep accurate financial records is to use accounting software with provisions for most if not all, your financial needs. Examples are listed in this chapter under the "Financial Tracking: Where Every Penny Goes" section.

Ink It In: Documenting Agreements and Transactions

When starting and growing a business, you cannot afford to leave any interaction or communication to chance. From the beginning, have everything in writing and always have a section for signing.

Whether communicating with other members, lenders, managers, vendors, or co-owners, ensure all parties sign. Essential documents to have signatures on include articles of organization, the operating document, certificate of good standing, loan or credit approvals, business contacts, and deals.

Secure Vault: Digital Data and Record-Keeping

Technology has helped businesses save on office space needed to keep records and documents. Record keeping has been made easier and more efficient because you can keep all documents online. Be it contracts, meeting minutes, financial statements, or operating documents, you can access them within seconds and on a single screen.

The earlier concern for security has been addressed with advanced features such as user permission and encryption. We recommend embracing digital data storage to enhance your company's security for record-keeping, save time, and become more organized.

Compliance Chronicles: Regulations and Taxation

An LLC must remain compliant with the regulations specific to the business structure and the tax requirements expected at the state and federal levels. Failing to comply may lead to hefty fines, penalties, or loss of the LLC status. Let's look at what regulation and taxation entail in LLC compliance.

Taxes: Understanding Obligations

Understanding an LLC tax obligation depends on whether you registered it as a single-member or multiple-member LLC. Using income tax obligation as an illustration, a single-member LLC will prepare a Schedule C document (issued by the IRS) to report its net income. That figure will be forwarded to your personal tax return to be taxed as a sole proprietorship. Conversely, for multi-member income tax reporting, you will be taxed as a partnership. Each partner will fill out a Schedule K-1 and then transfer the information to a single Schedule E document. Finally, each partner transfers their net income to their personal income tax return.

Regulatory Compliance: The Key to LLC Health

Regulatory compliance determines your LLC's health because failure to remain compliant with federal, state, or local laws may cost you the business or the LLC brand. Compliance also helps to maintain accountability and transparency in the daily business operations. It ensures you are up-to-date with the shifting economy and market needs. Besides, if you are compliant, anyone seeking to sue you will have a harder time proving their case. Regularly conduct an LLC-compliant audit to maintain your LLC's health.

Reporting Reality: Annual Reports and Statements

Submitting an annual report for your LLC is a requirement in most states. This document should contain details of all your business activities in the previous year and your financial performance. The annual report must be submitted on the anniversary of your LLC formation or a specific date set by the state. Even though you have all the records for submission, you must visit your Secretary of State website and download an annual report form, fill it out, and submit it with the required attachments or send it via mail.

Sales Tax Simplified (if applicable)

Most states require you to collect sales taxes. However, some local authorities offer sales exemptions depending on the type of product and point of sale. As you start operations, you must know when and how to charge sales tax—following your state's requirements. After registration for sales tax collection, find an efficient method to document the sales tax collected daily, weekly, or monthly. As the filing date approaches, gather the entire sales tax record and file the returns according to your state's specifications.

Licenses and Permits Unleashed

Most businesses require more than one license to operate. The number you need depends on the type of business, state rules, and location. So, which ones do you need? We provide an answer below.

License Quest: Identifying Your Needs

Once you develop your vision, mission statement, and goals, you are probably sure of the business you want to conduct and the extent to which you will go. Using that information, you should identify your business needs and the licenses and permits you should acquire. Examples that most businesses require include:

- County permits for sensitive businesses

- State licenses for most occupations

- Federal licenses for businesses regulated by the federal government

- Specialty city permits if you use special materials that can be a risk to the public

Permit Power: Applying with Confidence

Acquiring a permit gives you the right to operate a business in a specific location [8]. It is a powerful document to have as it silences anyone who comes to dispute your right to operate in a particular locality or sell certain products or services. The power you'll receive from this document should encourage you to apply for it with confidence. As long as you've done your homework and followed our recommendation in this beginner guide, you should approach this task with assurance that you'll get the permit to operate your business.

Renewal Rhythms: Staying in Compliance

As you get your licenses and permits, confirm how often you need to renew. Some business permits and licenses do not need renewal once you get them; others have an expiration date and require you to apply for a new one, or you may have to close your business or pay fines. Every state and locality differs in how often you need to renew your licenses and permits. Some expire after one year, while others go for a longer period. Keep track of all the permits and licenses to stay compliant.

Local Legends: Industry-Specific Licensing

As the name implies, industry-specific licenses are those business

licenses issued by industries specialized in an area of operation. These licenses ensure the person and the business meet particular criteria needed in that industry. For example, lawyers need certification from their state bar association. The federal, state, or private organizations (given a go-ahead by the state) issue the industry-specific licenses. Research carefully and ensure you meet all the requirements outlined.

Key Takeaways

- Members take full responsibility for the day-to-day running of the business in member-based LLCs, while managers perform the daily errands in manager-based LLCs.

- The best business bank account for an LLC offers tools to simplify tax and bookkeeping matters, refund or eliminate common fees, and provide opportunities to receive money back on some business purchases.

- Learning how to plan for taxes and adopting effective tax payment strategies will save you some money.

- Regulatory compliance determines your LLC's health because it helps to maintain accountability and transparency in daily business operations.

- Embrace digital data storage to enhance your company's security for record-keeping, save time, and become more organized.

- Some business permits and licenses do not need renewal once you get them, while others have an expiration date and require you to apply for a new one.

Chapter 5

Financing and Funding Your LLC

"Money is like gasoline during a road trip. You don't want to run out of gas on your trip, but you're not doing a tour of gas stations."
-Tim O'Reilly

Launching Your Business Finances

You entered into business to make money, but you must use what you already have well before you hit the target you had in mind. Having a business idea, identifying a target market, and noticing a need you can meet is not enough to realize your dream. You need money to put things in motion. Let's look at how to do it right.

Unmasking Startup Costs: Unveiling the Initial Expenses

Before choosing the method to finance your business, you must calculate how much money you will likely need for startup costs and unavoidable expenses. The initial step is to list all the expenses you will likely incur before and after you start operations. The following table categorizes these expenses and gives you examples.

Type of Expense	Examples
One time expenses	Equipment, machinery, or vehicles
	Incorporation fees
	Permits and licenses
	Computer or technology equipment
	Initial inventory and office supplies
Ongoing expenses	Utilities
	Marketing materials
	Office Supplies and operating expenses
	Website hosting and maintenance
	Business taxes
Fixed expenses	Lease or mortgage
	Insurance
	Utilities
	Administrative costs
Variable expenses	Inventory
	Payroll
	Shipping
	Packaging

Navigating Year One: Estimating Operational Costs

Once you've created a list of all the expenses you will incur, it's time to research and get the average cost of each item. For example, consult the registration agency to determine how much you need to register an LLC and get the necessary licenses. Shop around for the office equipment, furniture, and supplies you need, and take the most affordable ones. Further, set a certain percentage aside for other expenses like business taxes and utility charges that you may not know exactly how much you'll spend until the end of the month or quarter.

Safety Net Essentials: Contingency Planning for Unexpected Expenses

Regardless of how well you research and get your estimates, always expect to experience some setbacks or delays that may require you to use more cash. Factor in these unforeseeable expenses by adding cushion money. Some ongoing expenses may also increase as the months progress, so have some amount in the budget for these additional expenses.

Besides, it is important to ensure you have enough money to sustain the business for 6 to 12 months without expecting the business to fund itself. This is not to say that your business will not make money, but at this point, you cannot predict your sales until you start operating for a few months.

Funding Expedition: Your Path to Capital

Your financial strategy is in place, and you know where the money will go as you open your doors for business. Now, you need to have the money in your pocket to get started. Funding your LLC requires you to pull money from various avenues [9]. The following sections explore four sources.

Self-Funding and Bootstrapping: Starting Lean and Strong

The first place to look into to fund your business should be your own finances. New entrepreneurs often get money to start by liquidating their assets or using their possessions as collateral for loans. You may also go to the extent of using your personal savings or selling your property.

However, you must be careful when you dive deep into your personal assets. You risk losing your possessions if your business fails and you have taken a loan with your home, car, or land. To reduce the risk of losing your personal belongings if things go south, plan to make regular payments back to yourself. The main advantage of self-funding is that you have complete control of the business and do not have to answer to investors.

The Borrower's Route: Unraveling Debt Financing (Loans & Credit)

The traditional route of applying for loans from credit unions and banks is also an alternative to funding your LLC. Unfortunately, most lenders are reluctant to give their money to new businesses. So, be prepared to be rejected on multiple occasions. However, you can improve your chances of getting the loan by including your assets as collateral. LLC's safety net of having limited personal liability protects you from creditors accessing your assets if you fail to make the loan payments.

Another relatively similar way of getting a loan is through peer-to-peer lending websites. These online platforms allow you to apply for a loan.

Afterward, interested institutions or individuals decide whether to lend you the money and pay it back at an agreed interest rate. Examples of these sites are Prosper, Funding Circle, and Upstart.

The Investor's Pitch: Equity Financing (Angel Investors & VC)

Looking for individuals or entities to invest in your company and relinquish a percentage of your ownership is a route many entrepreneurs use to kick-start their business or grow it to new heights. Two main options for equity financing are looking for angel investors or venture capitalists.

Angel investors usually give a lower amount for a smaller percentage of the company, while venture capitalists offer more money, and you must give a higher percentage of your business. In addition, angel investors come in to help in the early days of your business, while venture capitalists come in later when they see your company has undeniable potential for growth.

A Crowd-Pleasing Alternative: Crowdfunding and More

Crowdfunding as a funding option entails asking people to donate to your LLC either online (Kickstarter or Indiegogo) or in person. Online tends to work better because you have a wider reach of people who may be willing to support you. You not only ask for money but also promise a reward for some, if not most, of your fund supporters.

To succeed with this approach, you must have a captivating marketing approach. You must also keep in mind that you may not get all the money you need for the startup. In most sites, you must wait until the crowdfunding campaign is over to access the funds. Use this approach if all other fundraising options are not available to you.

The Art of Bootstrapping

Can you start a successful business without relying on outside investments other than your personal finances? As business owners who have actually done it, we believe you can. Bootstrapping requires you to maximize the finances you already have to start and run your business. Here are the ways you can do it right.

Thrifty Tactics: Strategies for a Frugal Beginning

As you think of bootstrapping, consider carefully how your business will run with limited funds for the first few months of operations. Do not overcommit the little funds you have or overpromise your potential customers. The following are strategies to implement:

- Create a business plan with a very specific financial budget

- Determine how your revenue will cycle back to the business before paying yourself back

- Establish where additional resources will come from. For example, your own cash, borrow from your personal line of credit or use your time instead of employing someone.

- Plan to limit business operations. For example, only produce products upon order.

Penny-Wise Promotion: Cost-Effective Marketing

Working with a tight budget requires you to refine your marketing strategies. You want to get your business out there and become well-known, but do so in a way that'll have a high ROI for your business. To save on marketing, you need to consider the four main areas that can be affected by marketing and how to approach them. Let's illustrate with a table.

Marketing Aspect	What to Consider	Result
Product	Producing a good quality product or service with features that meet the customers' needs	The product or service will sell itself without over-advertising
Price	Choose a price that is not too high but also not too low to prevent you from making a profit	The product or service will sell itself without over-advertising
Place	Find out where your potential customers are and advertise on those platforms	Reach more people with less expenses compared to non-specific advertising
Promotion	Know what will captivate your potential customer and do exactly that.	More effective marketing with a targeted approach

Dollars and Sense: Efficient Resource Management

Efficient resource management ensures all the resources are used correctly and for the right projects or needs. Scrutinizing how the financial resources are used ensures you achieve your objectives even with limited funding available. You accomplish this by:

- Having all the information on a centralized platform to get a holistic approach and notice gaps.

- Assigning available resources to areas that need immediate attention.

- Distributing your resources across all areas instead of focusing on one area.

- Checking if there are new and more affordable resources to meet the same business need at a lower cost.

Tightening the Purse Strings: Mastering Cash Flow

To master cash flow, you need to know what happened to your LLC's money last month and what will happen to your cash in the coming days. This ensures you notice when you start bleeding cash and what you can do to recover. For instance, you'll know when to negotiate with your customers to make payments earlier than they want to commit. Or ask lenders to allow you to delay payments until a certain future date.

Attracting Angels and VC Wizards

As you seek to bring in investors, remember that not everyone who shows you the money is a great fit for your business. You first need to understand your business and the target market to know the kind of investor who will add value to it. Let's discuss how to win over the right investors.

Crafting a Captivating Pitch Deck

A pitch that captivates the investors highlights what you do, why you differ from similar businesses, and the problem you'll solve. You can also factor in brief financial figures and what customers or potential customers have said about your business. You may need to craft several pitch versions specific to various audiences, and always have a short 60-second point at your fingertips in case of an impromptu presentation.

Hunting for Investment Gold: Prospective Investors

As you try to find investors, you might realize that many focus on specific needs such as a business structure, industry, or under-represented founders. Regardless of the business they pick, they want to make revenue. They may not write big checks as from the start, but if you choose carefully, you can get investors to mentor you in running a successful business. However, they will not be involved in the daily LLC operations. You can find these investors through:

- Referrals and introductions
- Strategic networking
- Industry conferences and seminars
- Online investment platforms
- Cold outreach

The Art of Negotiation: Terms and Agreements

Investors seek to partner with someone who is not only after their money but is passionate about the business they are venturing into.

If possible, learn about the investor you are about to negotiate with and brainstorm some questions they might ask. When you enter the negotiating room [10], do not:

- Be quick to speak and preempt your terms.

- Assume you know what they mean; instead, ask questions to clarify.

- Overlook using your strengths as leverage.

- Use tricks or lies to win them over.

- Settle for less than you think your business is worth.

Sealing the Deal: Due Diligence and Closure

As with any important document, you must ensure that what you have in writing is what you agreed to in the meeting. Request more time to review the agreement you crafted with the investor during negotiations. Seek a lawyer's opinion to review the document or assist with amending the new agreement. You can also ask the investor for another meeting to discuss and clarify any ambiguous clauses. After that, confirm everything and sign the contract.

Leveraging Loans and Grants

Exploring loans or grants when starting your company or surviving a turbulent season is a viable option. The only difference between the two is that loans require repayments, whereas grants are one-time funding that you obtain from the government and non-profit organizations. Let's explore the vital aspects to know about loans and grants.

The Quest for Financing: Researching Options

Once you decide to either apply for a loan or a grant or use both methods, it is necessary to conduct relevant research on which lenders or grantors would be ready to give you the money. Look for unique grant opportunities targeted at your industry or those that your business will successfully address a need the government or NGO desires to meet. To get started, search online and in your locality for available grants in relation to your sector, tell your contacts about your plan to apply, and learn more from former grant recipients.

Paperwork Precision: Crafting Loan Applications and Proposals

Putting your thoughts, desires, and needs on paper can be more challenging than you think. You can put so much in the application proposal that you may be confused about what to add or leave. Don't worry, we got you covered. Here are the five elements you need to add to your loan application or proposal:

- Begin by giving an exhaustive description of your business and current financial situation.

- Explain why you need the loan and how it will assist you in meeting your goals.

- List assets you will include as collateral or security against the loan.

- Explain in detail how you plan to pay them back.

- Attach all supporting documents about your LLC, taxes, asset vs liability net ratio, balanced sheets, and bank statements.

Most grants do not require you to pay back the money, so you don't need to add a section on collateral assets or repayment plans, but you must include an exhaustive needs assessment, project description, and detailed budget.

Meeting the Requirements: Navigating Loan and Grant Expectations

Since loans are easier to get than grants, you are likely to get the loan approved if you add a collateral asset compared to not including any. Grants, on the other hand, are harder to get, so you must have an open mind. If you receive approval, the grant-giving agency will give you guidelines on how to use the funds and report its use. Loan lenders do not follow up on how you use the money as long as you repay them.

Financial Responsibility: Managing Repayments and Reporting

Loan repayments are usually straightforward because it entails keeping to what you agreed to in the contract and making timely payments. Ensure you do not miss payments or default because it will ruin your LLC's reputation with other lenders. In grant reporting, you are required to give a summarized narrative of the specific business project and a detailed financial report.

Ensure you provide the information you agreed to submit in the grant agreement you signed. Any changes from the original agreement should be reflected within the narrative section. Additionally, the narrative and the financial report should agree. For example, you cannot report you sold to 800 customers, and your sales report shows 920.

Key Takeaways

- Regardless of how well you research and get your budget estimates, always expect to experience some setbacks or delays that may require you to use more money.

- Most lenders are reluctant to give their money to new businesses. However, you can improve your chances of getting the loan by including your assets as collateral.

- Scrutinizing how the financial resources are used ensures you achieve your objectives even with limited funding.

- A pitch that captivates the investors highlights what you do, why you differ from similar businesses, and the problem you'll solve.

- Search for grants online or in your community, contact your networks to inform them of your plan, and talk to previous grant recipients about available opportunities.

Chapter 6

Nurturing Your LLC for Growth

"Test, measure, learn. It is the best way to understand what works best for your company and invest in the right area to become more efficient and achieve business growth."

-Irina Georgieva

Scaling Your LLC

After your business becomes a success and you are hitting your targets and meeting your goals, it is time to consider expanding. To succeed at scaling your business, you must ask yourself if you have the capacity to grow and to accommodate the growth. We will help you assess yourself and the business in this section.

Crafting Your Path to Sustainable Growth

Nurturing sustainable growth means that your business can support itself. It should give you reasonable profits, meet your customers' needs, and provide the employees with the support they need. The following are steps you can apply at an early stage to avoid serious scaling mistakes:

- Understand the changing customer needs and innovate to meet them.

- Implement well-defined processes addressing the rising needs.

- Monitor the changing industry dynamics and adopt or adjust as needed.

- Improve customer experience as the numbers increase.

- Ruthlessly monitor operations as targets and goals shift.

- Provide a healthy company culture with strong communication channels.

- Model integrity, honesty, and flexibility as the founder and business owner.

As you focus on these elements, remember to create brand loyalty so that your customers can stick by you even during challenging economic times.

Expanding Your Footprint: Products, Services, and Markets

Expanding your footprint involves creating a plan of action that will enable your business to grow its operations, add to its market share, and achieve the new scaling goals. Business expansion covers selling more of your products or services and entering new markets.

Expanding to new markets entails going into different geographical areas and opening new stores or establishing an online presence. Expansion in terms of products and services can involve creating a new product or service, licensing your product to other businesses, partnering with other companies, or repackaging your product or service to widen the reach.

Power Moves: Building Strategic Alliances and Partnerships

Strategic alliances and partnerships occur when two or more companies agree to work on a project together that will be of benefit to both parties. You may choose to enter such an arrangement to enable you to improve or sell more products or services, expand into a new market, or place yourself in a better position than your competitors [11].

Steps to form an alliance or partnership include brainstorming the kind of partners you'd like, how you'll approach the conversation, and drafting an alliance proposal that clearly shows how both parties will benefit. Once you get a company that agrees to the proposal, determine the goals together and devise a fair, profitable, and sustainable plan.

Crafting a Blueprint for Growth

When you launched your business, you created a blueprint for your startup. You ensured it captured your business needs and goals and had a strategic growth plan. Now, your business is growing, and you need to go back to the drawing board and create a new one or adjust the existing one to have a better business framework that will accommodate your growing business. We captured what you need to work on below.

Navigating Growth: SWOT Analysis and Strategy

In chapter two, we explained the meaning of SWOT analysis and outlined its parts in a table showing what each letter stands for and how it affects your business. You should also perform the same process with your growing business. Look at the strengths you've acquired over time. What are the weaknesses that are now preventing you from expanding more, which new and different opportunities are coming up as you grow, and what threats are you experiencing that will hinder you from further growth? Brainstorm and analyze these factors, then come up with a strategy to address each part.

Setting Sights on Success: Growth Goals and Milestones

It is often said that goals without milestones lack direction. Indeed, if you do not set clear milestones after you come up with your goals for the growing business, you will likely underachieve. Milestones are indicators that give you a picture of the growth process and help simplify your goals and objectives into manageable and easily identified day-to-day activities. After developing your goals, the milestones for each should contain four elements: description, date, budget, and delegation. These four elements will help you create clear and accurate direction for your team.

Turning Strategy into Action: Implementing and Monitoring Growth

Implementing and monitoring your growing business is the next step after developing a new business plan with specific goals and milestones. Implementation involves doing the work, while monitoring refers to measuring or tracking the numbers behind the implemented strategy. Below is a table that provides five ways of monitoring your business.

Monitoring Method	How it's Done
Live monitoring and testing	Looking at the live performance and the numbers as it happens
Reviews	Asking the customers about their experience with your business

Analytics Tools	Asking the customers about their experience with your business
Meetings and Appraisals	Asking the team directly about their views or analyzing individual performance
Market research	Comparing your current sales with the previous ones or with competitors

Adapt and Thrive: Fine-Tuning Strategies for Optimal Results

The first step in fine-tuning your business strategies is making sure you know everything about your new growth plan and how you wish to implement it. The following are examples of fine-tuning strategies you can use to ensure optimal results in your business:

- Refine your business goals and value proposition

- Enhance financial management

- Streamline operations and processes

- Evaluate competition and market trends

- Strengthen your sales and marketing approach

Getting optimal results for your business is not a one-time task. You have to keep monitoring, evaluating, and adjusting until you meet your target.

Beyond Borders and Boundaries

Doing business across states and internationally has been simplified by technology and efficient modern-day travel options. Even though logistically, things look manageable to expand beyond borders and boundaries. You must consider some key factors to succeed in it. Let's discuss more about it.

Franchise Fever: Taking Your Brand Nationwide

Taking your brand nationwide is a big step in your business journey that is worth celebrating. However, you must think through it carefully to ensure the timing is right and the approach will favor your success. Here are some steps to consider as you think about franchising:

- Find out what drove you to consider expanding.

- Generate a tailored strategy that would work in a new location

- Create a schedule of activities and add timelines

- Create an appealing portfolio of your products or services

- Open accounts at the new location

Locations, Locations, Locations: The Art of Expansion

The location where you intend to operate plays an essential role in determining whether the business will grow immediately after opening. The site you pick should be dictated by the kind of business you are engaged in and your own needs. The following are tips to help you choose the right location:

- Choose a location that fits your budget

- Factor in the location of the potential suppliers and vendors

- Establish your store where your products and services are in demand

- Consider transportation and accessibility for your employees

- Choose a safe location with ample spaces to park

Branching Out: Diversifying Your Offerings

Diversification is about making your presence felt in a new place after offering your products or services and increasing your profits in the process. Diversification can take several forms. For instance, you can diversify horizontally by introducing a new product or service to the market. The product can be in line with what you already offer or a totally different product with no relation to what you have. Vertical diversification entails adding a product that relates to what you already offer. For example, a salon offering hair services can decide to add a section for selling hair products.

Worldwide Ambitions: Considerations for Global Expansion

Expanding worldwide is a whole different ball game that requires you to take all precautionary measures before embarking on that journey. The following table presents the factors to consider before expanding globally.

Global Expansion Factor to Consider	What it Entails
Affordability	Include additional expenses such as international travel and customs
Employment and tax requirements	Different countries have their own requirements for employment and

	taxation regulations
Currency	Trade rate may fluctuate, making it hard to fix your costs to the international conversion scale
Financial and political unpredictability	Can make or break your new business when a serious crisis occurs in another country

Your marketing strategies will also change to align with the culture and preferences of the new region. You may need to form local partnerships from the onset to get it right.

Building a Winning Team

Building a winning team is a challenging process that requires commitment and a desire to invest in people. Merely having a group of talented employees does not automatically make them a winning team. You must put additional effort into the entire recruiting and retention process. We will discuss how you can build a winning team below.

Scouting Talent: Recruiting and Hiring the Right Way

Recruiting and hiring the right people is a critical task for ensuring adequate business growth. The right team ensures the company reaches its targets in terms of growth, maximizes productivity, provides better customer services, and enhances creative ideas. Follow these steps to increase your chances of getting the right team:

1. Outline your hiring requirements and create a precise job description.

2. Advertise on the most appropriate job posting site or work with a recruiting company.

3. Go through resumes and focus on who stands out.

4. Create a unique interview plan and ask the questions that matter to you.

5. Contact the references and perform background checks.

6. Choose the most appealing candidate and make an offer.

7. Onboard the new team member after negotiating the salary.

Onboarding Excellence: Setting Employees Up for Success

When you onboard new employees well, you set them up for success when they connect with coworkers, have a better grasp of the workplace culture, and get a deeper understanding of their new responsibilities. To ensure you get these three variables right, here are factors to have in place:

- Connecting them with relevant and friendly mentors during onboarding

- Ensuring the manager or supervisor is present and helpful

- Introducing them to employees on their department or floor

- Assigning someone to show them how things work

- Asking for feedback to know when they feel isolated or confused

Keeping Stars in Your Constellation: Employee Retention

Employee retention occurs when your hired team chooses not only to stay in your company but is also not actively looking for another job.

When you keep talents for longer, you are able to maintain uninterrupted business flow, enhance productivity, and reduce the costs of hiring. To retain your employees, you must give them challenging work, train them in other disciplinary skills as they hone their core skills, and develop a succession plan with them. You can encourage poor performers to step up by identifying why they are performing poorly and addressing the skills gap immediately.

Playing by the Rules: Legal Compliance and HR Mastery

Ensuring your company remains legally compliant in terms of human affairs requires you to have HR mastery. This means working with an HR manager who pays close attention to matters like recruitment, productivity, and retention [12]. They also monitor the employment laws to ensure your company adheres to all guidelines, including payroll, benefits, risk and safety, hiring, employee relations, and termination.

However, early on as your business grows, you may need to handle the HR duties yourself.

Adapting and Thriving

As seasoned business owners, we can confirm that your business will face a few shake-ups, be it from new regulations, the competitive landscape, or a national crisis. You need to learn from an early stage how to adapt to changes. We will explain more in the following paragraphs.

Market Watch: Staying Ahead of Trends and Shifts

A key area you must monitor to stay ahead is your market. The changes in the market include changing customer habits, the evolving business environment, and innovations that may threaten or improve your business. For example, artificial intelligence is here to stay, and you must keep innovating and finding creative ideas that you can work along with it or rise above it with the human qualities it lacks. Anticipating shifts and noticing new trends will help you make strategic decisions, such as training employees to acquire the skills to adapt to the change, improving the product or service, and looking for partnerships for reinforcement.

Flexible Foundations: Pivoting Your Business Model

Pivoting your business models involves changing an aspect of your company after realizing your product or services fail to meet the current or emerging needs of the market. Pivoting can help your company survive in the market and improve your revenue. Selcuk Atli, Co-founder of Bunch, came up with five pivoting areas that follow a standard order.

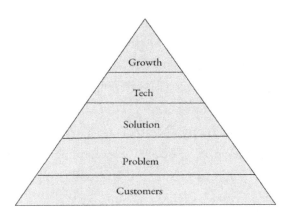

Selcuk asserts that pivoting requires you to understand if the customers are the issue (targeting the wrong group), you misinterpreted the problem you are trying to solve with your product or services, you are offering the wrong solution to the right or wrong problem, and your technology choice is working against your business. Once you address the factor causing a challenge, you'll experience growth.

Crisis Control: Navigating Stormy Waters with Grace

Whether you plan for it or not, a crisis is likely to occur at some point in your LLC. It may be internal (among members or employees) or external (with vendors, customers, or state regulators). To navigate the stormy waters with grace, you must put in place a crisis management plan that outlines who will take action when a specific crisis occurs and what their role entails. The goal of dealing with any crisis is to limit the harm done and restore normal business operations. Once you realize there is a crisis, pick a team to assess the crisis and determine the impact. Afterward, devise a plan for response, implement it, review it, and adjust until the crisis is over.

Lessons from the School of Hard Knocks: Gaining Wisdom from Failures

Failing in business is often inevitable. You will try some things and realize they don't work, or you may even make a loss from it. But failing provides a learning experience that can help you succeed. Keep in mind that when you fail, you must have gotten something wrong. Find out what it was, and research on it. Next, devise a plan to recover and ensure you train your team or have a policy surrounding it to avoid the same mistake. Indeed, failure isn't the end of your company. It is a slight setback on your journey to achieving your goals.

Key Takeaways

- Nurturing sustainable growth means that your business can support itself by making reasonable profits and meeting customers' needs.

- Milestones are indicators that give you a picture of the growth process and help simplify your goals and objectives into manageable and easily identified day-to-day activities.

- Diversification can be done horizontally by introducing a new product or service to the market or vertically by adding a product that relates to what you already offer.

- To retain your employees, you must give them challenging work, train them in other disciplinary skills, and develop a succession plan with them.

- To navigate a crisis, you must have a crisis management plan that outlines who will take action when a specific crisis occurs and what their role entails.

Chapter 7

Navigating the Legal Landscape

"Our goal is to set the gold standard when it comes to compliance."
-Cathy Engelbert

Crafting Contracts that Seal the Deal

Contracts help safeguard your business against legal issues and ensures both parties remain committed to the agreement. In business, all contracts must include some basic requirements to ensure they are legally enforceable and binding. We will explore more in the next section.

Drafting Effective Business Contracts

Effective business contracts should be able to communicate clearly to both parties and, at the same time, include all legal clauses to make said contracts enforceable. Striking a balance between the two needs can be challenging, especially with the constant change in regulations and business dynamics. Here are some tips to ensure you do it write:

- Include the relevant stakeholder's information.

- Define the purpose of the contract using simple and understandable language.

- Add important legal and business terms that ensure both parties understand their obligations and rights.

- Explain what each party is required to do and include a timeline.

- Review and edit the document to ensure you address all issues.

Unpacking the Different Types of Contracts

The diverse nature of doing business requires you to have a significant number of contracts that tackle issues in all departments. These contracts may have a similar outline, but the content should focus on what you seek to address. The following table presents some common types of contracts that are important to have.

Type of Contract	What's Involved
Sales contract	Contains sales and purchase information. It covers price, condition of items, warranty, and delivery
Employment contract	Outlines the relationship between an employee and employer and addresses the terms of employment
Service contract	An agreement entered by the client and service provider explaining the service to be offered, duration, patent terms, and obligations
Lease contract	Outlines your rights and those of your landlord, maintenance responsibilities, length of tenancy, and termination conditions

Partnership agreement	Addresses the relationship you'll have with your business partners. It includes profit-caring agreements and decision-making powers and processes

Mastering the Art of Contract Negotiation

Knowing how to negotiate a contract can determine whether you get the best or worst deal for your business. The company's size is less important than knowing the components and process of contract negotiations. Here are the steps to follow:

1. Understand what's at stake. How will the contract you are about to enter affect your company, relationships, and overall success?

2. Research and gather information about the parties involved, market trends, regulatory factors, industry standards, and legal implications.

3. Define your goals. Why do you want to enter this contract? Make sure you establish a reasonable standard you are unwilling to compromise, but do not ignore the reality.

4. Know your limits. What are the non-negotiables? How much can you push the other party before they walk away? You should remain firm but avoid destroying a possible cordial working relationship.

To succeed, build a strong negotiation team and prepare well by delegating who will address which issues.

Guarding Your Intellectual Fortunes

Guarding your intellectual fortunes entails keeping your company's information and secrets confidential. It also requires you to get copyrights on key aspects to ensure third parties don't steal your concepts, leaving you with a shell of a business. Let's discuss the key areas you need to guard.

Trademarks, Copyrights, and Patents: A Shield for Creativity

Trademarks, copyrights, and patents offer additional and long-term protection to your company that some contracts may fail to address. Copyrights do a good job of protecting your creative work by preventing anyone from using your work in your lifetime and some years afterward.

Patents come in to protect your inventions. You get the exclusive right to produce the product or use certain processes for your business only. However, you have to go through a somewhat complex process to apply, and you must prove the uniqueness of the product or process. Trademarks shield your company's name or symbol from being used by forgers or fraudsters to sell products or services in your company's name.

Safeguarding Your Brand: Protecting Names, Logos, and Products

Safeguarding your brand requires you to implement strategies and processes that protect your company's name, logo, and products. The risks involved when you fail to protect your brand include trademark infringement, brand dilution, counterfeiting, reputational damage, and cybersquatting [13]. Three ways to safeguard your brand include:

- Registering your trademark with key authorities.

- Using tools to monitor your brand in the marketplace.

- Taking legal measures against those who infringe on your brand.

- Registering your domain name and securing your online presence.

Vigilant Enforcement of Intellectual Property Rights

Protecting your rights as a creator, inventor, or business owner requires you to take legal action against the guilty party. As you vigilantly seek and take action against intellectual property infringers, you deter others from repeating the same mistake.

The most effective approach to vigilant enforcement is targeting the distributors rather than the consumers. Some customers may not be aware they are victims of pirated or fake products or services. Addressing it at the consumer level will not bear much fruit as opposed to taking the time to find the main suppliers and filing a case against them.

Shielding Your Business from Legal Storms

Part of the risk of starting any business is the likelihood of facing various legal storms coming from non-compliance, breach of contract, and failure to meet customers' demands. You can prepare ahead of time for some risks, while others come when you least expect them. So, how do you navigate legal storms? Let's answer your question below.

Defending Against Liability in an LLC

As we have discussed earlier, an LLC protects you and the members from personal liability in case your company goes into debt, or a creditor or customer files a lawsuit against you. However, this doesn't mean you can operate as you wish. The two situations that can remove this solid defense of an LLC are listed below.

- You, or a member, pierce the corporate veil by failing to follow the company's formalities, mixing your personal and business assets, or transferring personal or business assets as an individual instead of an LLC.

- When the owner, member, or employee commits a wrongful act.

Taking part in these activities weakens your defense against a lawsuit.

Safeguarding Your Assets with Comprehensive Insurance

Having comprehensive insurance coverage for your business protects you from losing your investment due to issues or risks you could not have avoided. Taking several insurance coverages can assist you in protecting your finances, ensuring you remain compliant, giving you peace of mind, and enhancing your company's credibility. Although it may be impossible to take all the covers available, the following are a few you can choose from:

- General Liability Insurance

- Property Insurance

- Commercial Auto Insurance

- Professional Liability Insurance

- Workers' Compensation Insurance

- Cyber Liability Insurance

- Product Liability Insurance

- Business Interruption Insurance

- Key Person Insurance

- Proactive Risk Management for Minimal Exposure

For a proactive approach to managing or avoiding already existing and future risks in the company, a risk management system should be considered [14]. It gives you speedy adaptability when faced with a crisis or unwanted events. To ensure you proactively address risk as opposed to using a reactive approach, consider the following steps:

1. Identify possible risks in different situations.

2. Determine the nature of the risk that motivates its occurrence and determine its root cause.

3. Determine how likely it is to happen and measure the possible effects to aid prioritization.

4. Have an open dialogue with experienced risk managers and skilled employees to help you prepare a contingency plan.

Think about adopting technological approaches such as real-time monitoring and regular reporting to reduce risk gaps in operations among various divisions.

Resolving Disputes with Finesse

Whether it's a disagreement due to a customer complaint or between partners, handling conflict is part of the package of running a business. Dealing with disputes can be expensive, time-consuming, and stressful, but here are important aspects to consider to ease the blow.

Alternative Dispute Resolution (ADR): Your Path to Harmony

Alternative Dispute Resolution (ADR) allows disagreeing parties to use other means of resolving conflict outside the courts. It offers an opportunity to deal with disputes without going through court processes that can be expensive, long, and time-consuming. Examples of ADRs are:

- Mediation

- Arbitration

- Facilitation

- Early neutral evaluation

- Settlement conferences.

The intention of ADRs is to develop a settlement or an agreement plan that addresses the issues defined by the parties involved.

Litigation and Legal Defense: When All Else Fails

Sometimes, parties in conflict may fail to reach an agreement after attempting to solve the matter using ADR methods. What follows is that the most aggrieved party will file a lawsuit against the other party. Litigation should be the last resort because the decision made in court can and will affect your company. Hence, ensure you have explored all means possible to settle the dispute.

In litigation, you or the other party files a lawsuit, and each responds. Next, you go for the motion hearing, where parties make requests to the judge. The discovery process is the next stage, where parties exchange evidence. Afterward, the pretrial takes place, followed by the trial, and then the judge makes a ruling, which is enforced—if there's no appeal.

The Art of Mediation and Negotiation

Knowing what to say and having facts regarding your matter isn't enough to ensure you get your issues addressed fairly during mediation or negotiation. You have to prepare and learn the art of dealing with surprises that often arise at the bargaining table. Mastering mediation and negotiation is knowing how to adapt to the changing dynamics while remaining focused on the desired outcome. Qualities you need to bring to negotiations and mediations include:

- Approach the negotiation seeking to harmonize interests.

- Be patient.

- Understand the issues from both sides.

- Listen carefully before thinking of a response.

- Be respectful.

When to Seek Legal Counsel: Tips for Hiring an Attorney

In most situations, you can resolve your disputes without the need to hire an attorney. But some occasions may warrant seeking legal counsel, such as when the dispute becomes too complicated if the other party uses a lawyer whose terms you may not clearly understand, when the case goes to litigation, and when you don't want to risk worsening the situation by using your limited legal knowledge. Some tips for hiring a competent attorney are:

- Ask for recommendations or search online.

- Research about the attorney's experience and reviews.

- Schedule appointments with several attorneys.

- Prepare the questions you want to ask.

- Assess fees and compare with the likely candidates.

- Choose the attorney you can afford and is most compatible.

Remember to sign an agreement stipulating all the services they will render to you. Do not make assumptions. Put it in writing.

Staying on the Right Side of the Law

As business owners with some degree of experience, we know that staying compliant is like aiming at a moving target. There are increased reporting requirements, ever-changing and complex rules and requirements, rapid technological changes, and constant regulatory scrutiny. You may feel overwhelmed, but with a proper mindset and team, you can stay on the right side of the law. Let's address key concerns.

Navigating Tax Compliance and Reporting

Staying tax compliant has always been an area that most businesses struggle with. The process can be draining and turn punitive if you miss an entry or a deadline. You risk being financially exposed, tarnishing your brand image, or disrupting operations.

Implement the following to ensure you do not miss a crucial figure while reporting or overlook a filing date:

- Put efficient systems in place that identify and address tax risks.

- Have appropriate tax policies and have them explained to relevant parties.

- Use technology to ease the process of gathering and reporting taxes.

- Ensure you keep updated records and accurately report them.

The Labyrinth of Employment Laws and Regulations

As a reputable LLC company, you must acquire knowledge about employment rules and regulations. Observing factors such as minimum wage, compensations, anti-discriminatory regulations, and workplace safety ensures you provide a healthy workplace with little or no legal loopholes. The following table outlines some key state and federal areas in which you must remain updated and compliant.

Employment Regulatory Laws	What it Addresses
Equal Employment Opportunity (EEO) Laws	Discrimination
Occupational Safety and Health Administration (OSHA)	Workplace safety
Legal employment contracts	Fairness in employment
Fair Labor Standards Act (FLSA	Wage payment and child labor
Family and Medical Leave Act (FMLA)	Job-protected leave

In addition to adhering to these laws, you should have an employee handbook that every employee must read and understand the company's policies and procedures.

Green Business: Environmental and Industry-Specific Compliance

Green businesses, also referred to as sustainable businesses, aim to ensure companies make a profit but also work at preserving the planet's health. Becoming a green business requires adopting sustainable practices, such as those listed below.

- Producing environmentally friendly products.

- Increasing the use of renewable energy.

- Reducing waste by recycling.

- Finding legal ways of sourcing labor and materials.

- Using sustainable packaging.

Governments are increasingly requiring companies to implement developing laws and regulations surrounding sustainability. Research

these laws in your industry and implement them where applicable.

The Ongoing Challenge of Compliance Monitoring and Updates

Undoubtedly, monitoring compliance comes with various challenges that arise from the tools, individuals, or processes used to get the job done. For example, employees may spend hours each week creating and adjusting reports for the LLC members, and that is time they would have used to be more productive. Other challenges involved in compliance include:

- Lack of resources (financial, human, or technical).

- Failing to use modern automated processes and continuing with manual methods.

- Minimal accountability until the last minute.

- Complex regulatory requirements.

- Disconnected systems that fail to work together to prevent or address emerging compliance issues.

If these challenges become overwhelming, consider working with professionals to streamline everything. Afterward, let them train the members and employees on how to monitor and stay updated on compliance matters.

Key Takeaways

- Effective business contracts should be able to communicate clearly to both parties and, at the same time, include all legal clauses to enforce them.

- The most effective approach to vigilant enforcement against intellectual property infringement is targeting the distributors rather than the consumers.

- Litigation should be the last resort because the decision made in court can and will affect your company. Ensure you have explored all ADR options.

- To improve your company's ability to manage or avoid existing and emerging risks, consider having a proactive risk management system.

- Green business aims at ensuring companies make a profit but also works at preserving the planet's health.

Do you want to make sure you avoid any mistakes when getting your LLC going? Check out our free guide on The 5 Mistakes Beginners Make When Starting Their LLC. Just go here to download it now: **www.LLCLegend.com**

Chapter 8

Navigating LLC Taxes

"The legal right of a taxpayer to decrease the amount of what otherwise would be his taxes, or altogether to avoid them, by means which the law permits, cannot be doubted."

-George Sutherland

Deciphering Tax Complexity: LLCs Unveiled

A primary reason business prefer starting as an LLC is the tax benefit that comes with it. Unlike corporations, LLC permits business owners to pay taxes once. This section explains this advantage and discusses other critical tax information.

Unraveling Pass-Through Taxation

Pass-through taxation occurs when an entrepreneur pays taxes on LLC income after it is distributed to the owners as wages or an investment return. This means that each LLC member must report the company's income and losses on their personal income tax return. In the IRS records, an LLC is treated as a disregarded entity for tax purposes, meaning the LLC has no obligation to pay taxes and does not exist outside the owners.

Slight variation occurs in the method of taxation depending on whether the LLC is a single-member or a multi-member. An LLC owned by one person pays taxes as a sole proprietorship and reports income and losses on personal tax returns. While an LLC with multiple owners can be taxed as a partnership, corporation, or S-corporation. The default method is a partnership.

Unveiling the Self-Employment Tax Quandary

Apart from your regular income tax, you are required to pay self-employment tax. For instance, as an employee, you would pay half of the Social Security and Medicare taxes and your employer the other half. But as a self-employed person, you must pay the entire amount.

Fortunately, there's a way to reduce the tax burden. Once you set up an LLC, you can choose to exist as a disregarded LLC and pay the self-employment taxes in full or elect to be taxed as an S-Corporation, which reduces the burden of paying self-employment tax. As an S-Corp, you pay yourself a salary, and the self-employment taxes will be deducted from there. Afterward, pay yourself other amounts as distributions from the S-Corp. This approach prevents you from paying self-employment taxes on that amount.

Tax Credits and Deductions Demystified

Interestingly, the IRS does not typically tax an LLC directly. Instead, profits are paid to members, who then file them on their personal tax returns. This is called pass-through taxation. Members then file personal income taxes, including the profits from the LLC. However, LLCs offer an advantage in flexible tax classification.

An LLC is not limited to pass-through taxation but can elect to file as an S corporation. If the LLC is classified as an S corporation, the LLC files a tax return as a separate entity. IRS Form 8832 Entity Class Election allows you to change the tax classification of the LLC. The benefits of an S corp classification include savings on Medicare and Social Security taxes since members gain employee status. This also allows members to avoid self-employment taxes. However, it may pose a double taxation issue as the LLC pays a corporate tax rate, and members pay personal income taxes on the income from the LLC. An experienced tax advisor can help you decide which tax status is best for your individual situation.

Mastery of Business Taxes: A Strategic Approach

Once you know how to lower the tax burden, the next step is mastering the taxation process, even if that means outsourcing to a tax professional. You can opt to take care of the tax requirements and obligations on your own or employ a tax professional to do it. Either way, the following section addresses what you need to know.

Tax Time Tactics: Filing for Your LLC

Filing taxes for your LLC depends on whether you are a single or multi-member LLC. The main difference is the IRS forms used. Let's look at the steps:

1. Prepare all the documents and have them ready.

2. Choose the right tax form. For a single-member LLC, you will use Schedule C. Add the income and expenses from the business in the form, then transfer the income or loss on your personal tax return Form 1040.

3. For multi-member LLCs, you must complete Form 1065 for

partnerships and Form 1120-S for an S-Corp. Afterward, you must provide a Schedule K-1 to each member. They should calculate their percentage income and transfer it to their personal tax return forms.

4. Next, fill out Schedule SE, which covers your self-employment taxes.

5. Calculate state and federal employment taxes if you have employees.

6. Consider any other state-applicable taxes.

The Art of Anticipating Quarterly Tax Payments

As a member of a business that operates as an LLC, you will likely owe quarterly taxes. Small businesses pay this type of tax in advance of their annual tax return. It operates on a pay-as-you-go basis where you pay throughout the year as estimations. Two main guidelines used to confirm whether you qualify to make quarterly tax payments are:

- You will owe more than $1,000 (after tax credit) when filing your return at the end of the year.

- Your withholding and tax credits will likely be less than 90% of your tax liability for the year.

Depending on what type of LLC you have - if you're a single member LLC, 1120S, or a Form 1065, you'll take that income and use it to calculate your quarterly income taxes on a Form 1040-ES. You're expected to file four times a year.

Deadlines and Extensions: Staying One Step Ahead

The deadline for paying your personal taxes from your LLC's income is April 15. However, if you elect to be taxed as a C-Corp or S-Corp, you must file your annual returns by March 15. Since you may also have quarterly payments, the deadline is as follows: April 15, June 15, September 15, and lastly, January 15.

The IRS penalizes you for filing late and failing to pay on time, even after filing before the deadline. Fortunately, the IRS allows you to file for an extension using Form 4868, but you must make the request before the tax return due date. If approved, you will receive an extension of six months. The IRS also allows you to get an extension by paying part or all of your income tax due and informing them that it's for an extension.

Tax Pro vs. DIY: Making the Right Choice

After interacting with the above information, you may feel overwhelmed by the requirements and forms needed to manage your taxes. You should consider hiring a professional to ease the burden if you have several sources of income and sizable assets. But if you have one stream of income and little to no deduction, then DIY is possible once you understand the requirements. Assess your situation and determine if DIY or hiring a tax professional will save you money in the long run.

Balancing the Books: The Accounting Odyssey

Balancing the books is the ultimate determinant of whether your business is worth remaining open. You can tell the general financial health of your company by looking at the financial records and transactions. So, what is involved in bookkeeping? We answer this question below.

Precise Financial Records: A Keystone for Success

Keeping precise financial records helps you assess your business profitability. It enables you to identify where your financial weaknesses and strengths lie. This action helps you to make informed decisions on investments, budgeting, and future growth strategies. The following are other ways accurate financial records set you up for success:

- Assist you in remaining tax compliant.

- Establish organizational trust and transparency.

- Ensure you detect fraud and errors.

- Keep you organized and efficient.

Cash vs. Accrual: The Accounting Dilemma

As a small business owner, you have the option of using cash or an accrual accounting system. The main difference is that accrual accounting registers expenses and revenue when a transaction occurs and without payment, while cash accounting registers the expenses and revenue when cash exchanges hands. The table below summarizes the key differences.

Cash Accounting	Accrual accounting
Records after receiving money	Records after a transaction
Less accurate for not recognizing unpaid items	More accurate as it gives an overall picture of business transactions
Ease to use	Complex because of multiple records for tracking payments

Preferred by small businesses	Serves larger companies better because of inventory

The Ledger Landscape: DIY or Pro?

Without a doubt, a general ledger can be a complex book to keep. It contains all your company's classified financial data and is recorded as debits and credits. It has various financial accounts such as owner's equity, assets, liabilities, revenues, and expenses. Do you think you can manage to keep up with all this information? It is possible for a small business, but if your business has undergone significant growth, hiring a professional accountant can save you time and energy and eventually save you some money when they streamline your accounts.

Tools of the Trade: Accounting Software Insights

Manual methods of tracking finances are no longer ideal in today's world. Lots of accounting software has been developed for small and large businesses. Using this software helps reduce human errors in record keeping, inventory, budgeting, and when handling account payables and receivables. These tools include Wave, Zoho, QuickBooks, FreshBooks, Xero, and Sage.

Dollars and Deductions: A Tax Odyssey

The IRS legally allows businesses to take advantage of available provisions that can save companies thousands of dollars through tax deductions. Make it part of your goal to learn about tax deductions and use them every time you file your taxes.

Tax Benefits Unveiled: Common LLC Deductions

As mentioned earlier, you can take advantage of tax deductions using various provisions that the IRS approves. These deductions are used to encourage businesses to grow and enable them to add benefits specific to employees without incurring additional costs in taxes. The following are examples of LLC deductions you can explore:

- Starting a business expenses

- Home office expenses

- Travel and vehicle expenses

- Business meals

- Education and medical expenses

- Business interest, bank fees, and insurance

- Rent expenses

- Professional Expenses

- Certain office supplies and utilities

Exploring the Frontier: R&D Tax Credits

The Research and Development (R&D) tax credit can be claimed by companies dedicated to coming up with new and improved business elements such as computer software, products, techniques, formulas, or inventions [15]. As a start-up, you can apply for the R&D tax credit against your payroll for up to five years. Your business could be eligible if you:

- Improve on existing products.

- Use your time and resources to produce new and innovative products.

- Come up with patents, prototypes, processes, or software.

- Hire scientists, designers, and engineers.

Opportunities Unlocked: The Work Opportunity Tax Credit (WOTC)

The Federal government offers the Work Opportunity Tax Credit (WOTC) to employers who hire people from a particular targeted group undergoing significant employment barriers. You can qualify to claim the WOTC for a person who falls under the following category of people:

- Formerly incarcerated or convicted of felony.

- Veterans.

- Resident of empowerment zones or rural renewal counties.

- A rehabilitated person.

- A person whose family is under state assistance or supplemental security income.

The Home Office Advantage: Deduction Details

As the name implies, home office deduction permits entrepreneurs doing business at their residential premises to deduct certain home expenses on their tax returns. These expenses include:

- Mortgage interest

- Utilities

- Repairs

- Maintenance

- Depreciation

- Rent

To qualify, you must be exclusively using a part of your home for operating your business regularly. Secondly, the home must be your principal place of running your business. However, if you have another location but conduct your administrative and management activities at home, you may still benefit from a home office deduction.

Expertise Beyond DIY: Tapping into Financial Professionals

Reaching this far into the guide, you may have noticed that you have significant work to do to get your LLC up and running. Not forgetting the changes you must implement as your company grows. The question on your mind could be, will you single-handedly manage all these tasks, or do you need to look for professionals? As you think about it, we will outline what you need to know about working with professionals.

Partnering with the Pros: Accountants and CPAs

At some point in your business, you will need to hire an accountant or

a CPA to manage your financial records. They can also assist you in planning your LLC business structure from the beginning. Having an accountant coming on board will help to keep complex tax information in check. The following table shows other duties a CPA or accountant can perform.

Accountant/CPA's Function	Benefit
Tax advice and planning	Save money on taxes and keep track of new legislation impacting taxation for your business
Management and consulting	Budgeting, preparing statements, and risk management
Audit and assurance	Addresses tax problems
Payroll administration	Ensures everyone is paid on time
Bookkeeping	Handles account receivables and invoices
Forensic accounting	Prevent or discover embezzlement or fraud

Financial Advisors: Your Trusted Navigator

The descriptor of "financial advisor" encompasses various financial professionals who can help your business succeed. A financial advisor can be an investment manager, stockbroker, financial planner, tax preparer, estate planner, and banker [16]. Generally, the financial advisor you work with should provide advice and guidance on a specific financial matter. They should be well-educated, experienced, and have the proper credentials. The person you choose should work on your behalf to ensure your business achieves its goals while maximizing its revenue.

Legal and Tax Gurus: Consultants for Clarity

A business that desires to stay compliant and take advantage of available legal and tax benefits must consult with an attorney or tax professional at some point. An experienced business attorney can assist you in:

- Creating and enforcing contracts.

- Ensuring asset, property, and cash protection.

- Preparing employment agreements.

- Enlightening you on tax laws.

- Guiding you on the closure of LLC or bankruptcy application.

A tax consultant comes in to guide you through tax return preparation and filing. They will also assist you to claim the deductions mentioned earlier. A tax guru will help you discover all the secrets the IRS makes it difficult for most businesses to know. The IRS has targets to meet, and they count on a complex tax code "hiding" some tax advantages and loopholes.

Empowering DIY: Resources for Financial Mastery

The DIY approach to operating and managing your business will be effective if you remain focused and organized. Financial stability and a positive cash flow are signs that you are going in the right direction. Tasks you need to add to your to-do list include:

- Budgeting

- Tax planning

- Forecasting

- Accounting

- Risk management

Don't let this list intimidate you. Diverse resources are available to simplify your work. They include accounting software like Quickbooks and Square, payroll software like Square Automatic Payroll, income tax software like TaxCloud and EasyOffice, and management tools like Monday.com and Wrike.

Key Takeaways

- The state or federal government does not require the LLC to pay taxes, but it passes through to the members' individual tax returns. However, some states, like Rhode Island, have an annual tax that must be paid.

- The members of an LLC are likely to owe quarterly taxes, depending upon the income received from the LLC.

- Keeping precise financial records helps you assess your business profitability and identify where your financial weaknesses and strengths lie.

- R&D (research and development) tax credit can be claimed by companies dedicated to coming up with new and improved business elements such as computer software, products, techniques, formulas, or inventions.

- A financial advisor can be an investment manager, stockbroker, financial planner, tax preparer, estate planner, banker, and accountant. They should provide advice and guidance on a specific financial matter.

Chapter 9

Navigating Transitions and Beyond

Selling Your LLC: The Art of Transition

What happens when you reach a point in your LLC where you feel it's time to sell? You can get to this point when you are approached with a good deal, you want to pursue a new venture, or you just want to retire. Selling your LLC needs careful planning and creating a business blueprint for a seamless transition. We look at how to go about it in this section.

Preparing Your LLC for Sale: Getting It Market-Ready

Ensuring your LLC is ready for sale involves studying your business and getting it market-ready. That means you must evaluate where buyers are at regarding service features and then add any missing elements to enhance the value of your company. The following are essential elements to work on to make your LLC market-ready:

- Evaluate your LLC's position by examining the financial statements.

- Evaluate the current market condition and improve your financial performance.

- Look into your existing working relationships and strengthen the bond.

- Analyze your competitors and how you can stay ahead.

Valuing Your Business: What's It Really Worth?

You define what you consider to be the worth of your business by assessing all areas of the company: capital structure, management, net book value (market value of assets), and net profit or loss. These factors estimate your company's value and assist you at the negotiation table. The three methods available for valuing your business are summarized in the table below.

Valuation Approach	How its Done
Asset-based approach	Gives a total of all your investments, determining your business' value. It's done by adding assets and subtracting liability
Earning value approach	Evaluate your business based on its ability to continue making wealth in the future
Marketing approach	Estimates your company's value by establishing what your business is worth by the price similar businesses sell for.

Finding Potential Buyers: The Search for the Perfect Match

Finding the right buyer for your business may take time. It involves putting your business up for sale physically or online and searching for the right buyers. Here are ways to find the perfect buyer that matches your needs:

- Network with people doing business in your niche, industry professionals, and associations

- Seek buyers online in various online communities and business platforms that can give you a wider audience.

- Hire a business broker, mergers and acquisition advisor, and legal or financial professional experienced in business transactions.

- Explore business broker sites such as Empire Flippers. They specialize in selling a business once it is established.

Negotiating the Sale: Sealing the Deal Gracefully

After you find the perfect buyer, you must enter the negotiating room with an idea of who the buyer is and how much you want from your business. The steps to follow as you prepare for negotiation are:

1. Gather information about your business, the current market, the buyer, and the company's projections.

2. Read and practice the negotiation strategies you need to use. Keep in mind your bottom line and other areas that are non-negotiables.

3. Negotiate the selling price by dividing your company into various parts.

4. Prepare the contingencies that must be implemented before completing the sale.

5. Talk to a business advisor to ensure you are making the right decision.

Passing the LLC Baton: Legacy Planning Unveiled

You may not want to sell your business as you retire or go on to another venture. A succession plan is an option to consider to keep your business legacy going. It involves choosing the right person or people to run your company [17]. Let's discuss how to do that.

Estate Planning and Succession: Ensuring Your Vision Lives On

Estate and succession planning brings together the aspect of preparing who will take over your business assets and also the leadership of the company. If you run a single-member LLC, you must transfer ownership and management rights to the next person. However, an LLC with multiple owners permits you to transfer your ownership rights, but the leadership roles must be discussed with all partners. In effecting your plan, you need to have clarity of thought in figuring out what is important to you vs. what is best for the company's future and then striking a balance between the two.

Grooming a Successor: Handing Over the Reins with Care

The successor you choose can take your business to new and better heights or jeopardize your business legacy and run it down. The journey to select a successor starts early, and the following are the tips you can use as you groom a successor:

- Identify, interview, and choose a suitable successor who wants to build your company and has the skills to do it.

- Identify and address skills and knowledge gaps the successor may have and work on a plan to rectify them.

- Document essential company processes and ensure they are aware of how things are done.

- Build a strong team that can help the successor achieve the company's goal.

Family Business Considerations: Balancing Blood and Business

Balancing blood and business is a sensitive undertaking because you do not want to appear to be giving special treatment to the family and risk losing trust with the employees or breeding resentment towards the blood successor. You must let your family successor work as hard as the other employees to earn their place as the successor. Using more of the merit instead of the inherit model helps to send a clear message that you are not handing over the company to someone who hasn't met the company's expectations. Even though your family members have a unique position, they must have good performance metrics.

Legal and Tax Implications of Succession: Navigating the Regulatory Maze

Legal or tax implications are a factor you must consider as you work on implementing your succession plan. Whichever approach you choose, you will have to part with some money to meet certain tax requirements. For legal implications, your main task will be updating business licenses, permits, and company documents and transferring contracts and liabilities. Tax implications include capital gain taxes for selling the LLC and gift or estate tax for transferring ownership. To minimize the tax implication, work with a professional who can help you qualify for exemptions and tax breaks.

Closing Down the LLC: A Strategic Farewell

Closing down your LLC ensures you do not accrue financial responsibilities after you've stopped operations. The processes involved notify the various authorities of your decision that all legal processes attached to your LLC should stop. We break down the key things to address as you close down.

Voluntary Dissolution Process: The Final Curtain Call

Voluntary LLC dissolution occurs when members agree to close down the company due to various reasons, such as the death of a member or hard economic times. The process is as follows:

1. Have a meeting to dissolve the LLC as per the operating agreement or state laws

2. File the articles of dissolution with your state authorities.

3. File the pending tax returns and pay all debts

4. Take care of pending contracts, sell agreed-upon assets, and distribute the rest

5. Follow any other procedure you included in the operating agreement.

Settling Business Debts and Obligations: Ending on Good Terms

Ending on good terms with your creditors or vendors is a professional and ethical way to handle your pending debts and obligations The creditors might even agree to a lower settlement in an attempt to get some money before you close down [18]. Fortunately, LLCs protect you from creditors seizing your assets, but those same creditors can come for your company's assets as a way to get a portion of their money. Try to work things out with them, as they have helped you keep your business doors open.

Distributing Assets to Members: Wrapping Up the Finances

Legally, distributing assets to members should not take place until you have settled all the debts with creditors. Afterward, the members can divide the assets according to the provisions outlined in the operating agreement. Take the following steps to distribute assets fairly:

1. Sell tangible assets for cash

2. Share out the gain or loss realized from the sale to partners (as per the income rations)

3. Pay liabilities in cash to the partners

4. Distribute the remaining cash on the basis of capital balances.

Filing Final Tax Returns and Compliance: The Last Chapter in LLC Life

As you close your LLC, one of the last vital steps is to file your final tax return and close all tax accounts with the IRS and state. If you have a payroll or sales tax account, ensure it is funded correctly and up to date. To close your IRS tax account, you must file a final Form 1065 if you run a multi-member LLC and Form 1040 for a single-member LLC. Ensure you check the final return box. The other members should also tick the final return box in their Schedule-K-1 form before transferring the income or loss to their personal tax return form. Finally, confirm with your local, county, and state authorities that you have complied with all the guidelines in closing an LLC.

Key Takeaways

- When planning to sell your LLC, you must assess the buyers' needs and meet those standards to optimize your company's value.

- Using more of the merit instead of the inherit model helps to send a clear message that you are not handing over the company to a family member who hasn't met the company's expectations.

- Closing down your LLC officially with various authorities ensures you stop accruing financial responsibilities when you cease operations.

Chapter 10

Unveiling Triumphs: LLC Case Studies

"Success isn't about what you accomplish in life; it's about what you inspire others to do."

-Anonymous

Industry Insights: Profiling Successful LLCs

As mentioned in earlier chapters, LLCs are the most favorable business structure for entrepreneurs starting a business. This section will share two stories of people who chose to form an LLC from the onset and how it worked out for them. Afterward, we will see the valuable insights you can gain from them and others.

Diverse Tales of LLC Triumphs

Our first story is that of Zach Ranen, founder of RAIZE bakery. He discovered a niche that enabled him to reinvent traditional cookies and modernize them to meet the current market trends. He researched the various business structures and chose to form an LLC. Zach did not want the cumbersome paperwork of a corporation but still wanted to protect his personal assets from liability when he expanded. He worked with a company that assists new entrepreneurs in forming LLCs and was advised to register his LLC in Delaware and qualify the LLC in New

York state. Within a short period, he was up and running as an LLC in New York.

Our second story is that of Brian Chesky and Joe Gebbia, the founders of Airbnb. They were undergoing financial challenges and decided to transform their apartment in San Francisco into a rental space. What started as a simple solution to their problem became a major online platform where people could make money by renting their spaces, and others would find affordable places to stay as they travel. Although it currently operates as a publicly traded company, its initial business structure was similar to that of an LLC.

Airbnb hosts often utilize the asset protection of LLC formations when operating their business. Establishing an LLC protects your personal finances and assets from financial penalties or legal actions that might result from hosting an Airbnb property.

Gaining Valuable Insights from Real-Life Stories

The above two stories and other success stories from famous LLC companies like Google LLC, Blackberry LLC, and eBay LLC have helped rising entrepreneurs gain insights into running their own LLCs [19]. These valuable insights include:

- Beginning small and keeping costs down to avoid depending heavily on outside funding.

- Understanding your area of expertise and narrowing it down until you find your unique selling point.

- Realizing when it's time to bring in an expert to help you set up your LLC to ensure you take care of all the legal and tax requirements.

- Knowing when to formalize the LLC to make sure you benefit from the tax benefits and personal asset protection.

- Calculate when you should pay yourself vs. put back the profits into the business to enable further growth.

- Realizing when it's time to change to another business structure to allow scaling into greater heights.

- Understanding the need to form meaningful work associations and create a warm, caring relationship with the customers.

Strategic Moves: Navigating Success

You will rarely find a successful LLC that does not have to apply particular strategies to get to the high-achieving level it operates on. For instance, they had to stop some activities and learn new ones. These success strategies required them to stay up-to-date with emerging trends and study their company's operational methods. Let's learn some of these strategies and discover other lessons picked by the pros.

Vital Strategies and Decision-Making That Paved the Way

As you have learned in the earlier chapters, having a business idea and the passion to start a business is not enough. You must think about, and research vital strategies to implement that pave the way for success. The following are strategies and decisions successful LLC owners had to consider in order to succeed:

- They clearly defined their niche, found their target market, and put all efforts into winning their ideal customers.

- They started with as little expenses as possible and minimized upfront fees while taking advantage of the available free or inexpensive resources.

- They accepted that technology is here to stay and found a way to use it to their advantage while adding a human touch where possible.

- They closely monitored their financial records, ensuring they remained disciplined and had significant cash reserves to address unavoidable crises.

- They made it their goal to establish a healthy company culture that addressed the employees' and customers' needs and held them in high esteem.

- They created systems to assist them in addressing arising challenges and take advantage of the flexibility LLCs offer.

Lessons Learned from the Pros

Let's learn directly from some of the famous people who started successful businesses and what their most important lessons are:

1. "Focus narrowly on excelling in one core competency vs trying to be everything to everyone." - Linda Findley Kozlowski, founder of Etsy (handmade goods marketplace)

2. "Obsess over the problems you are solving for your customers - not external validation or vanity metrics," said Katia Beauchamp, co-founder of Birchbox (beauty product sampling).

3. "Company culture and shared values define and unite a business - make them a priority starting day one." - Christine Tao,

founder of Sounding Board (business coaching).

4. "Obsess over customer experience and satisfaction - negative word of mouth can tank a small business." - Tristan Walker, founder of Walker & Company Brands (health and beauty products)

5. "Be frugal and bootstrap as much as possible in the early days to preserve control and flexibility," said Tobi Lütke, founder of Shopify (e-commerce platform).

6. "Focus on building a product or service that delivers outstanding value," said Sahil Lavingia, founder of Gumroad (e-commerce platform).

7. "Pay close attention to cash flow and financing from day one, managing budgets rigorously even during growth stages." - Jenn Hyman, founder of Rent the Runway (designer dress rental).

Overcoming Obstacles: LLC Challenges Conquered

As business owners, we have faced various challenges as we ran our businesses. We have also helped countless entrepreneurs overcome obstacles they have experienced as they began their businesses and in the growth process. Here is what we have to say about overcoming obstacles.

The Grit and Determination Behind Success

Grit is a quality most entrepreneurs should have because it helps you to keep going when things get tough. It propels you forward to achieve your business goals even when the outlook seems bleak. Entrepreneurs with grit motivate themselves to move forward. They do not view failure as the end but see it as a business approach that doesn't work [20]. It sets them forth to look for another strategy with the lesson they learned from the failure in mind. Ways to enhance your grit are:

- Improve your performance by setting goals and assessing your progress often.

- Focus on your passion and purpose when facing hardships.

- Accept failure and move on without beating yourself down.

- Develop attainable goals and be realistic about the outcomes desired.

- From a team to lean on when challenges come.

- Manage your emotions. Never get too high after the wins or too low after the losses. Stay even keel, and consistently move forward as you chart your path to success.

A Deeper Dive into Triumph Over Troubles

When going through changes in your LLC, you may feel like the troubles are too much, and you cannot see a way out or a sign of triumph on the horizon. You probably know there's nothing new under the sun, meaning countless entrepreneurs have gone through the troubles you are going through now. What set apart those who triumphed and those who remained in their troubles was their mindset. The following table compares the mindset of people who triumph sooner vs. those who stay in business troubles longer.

	Triumph Mindset	**Trouble Mindset**
Attitude	Optimistic and confident	Pessimistic and threatened
Planning	Strategic and adaptable	Rigid and stressed
Finances	Stabilizes reserves and controls costs	Erratic spending cuts
Resilience	Leverage challenges to get better	Demoralized by challenges
Focus	Sees opportunity	Sees obstacles

Learning from Legends: Key Takeaways

In this chapter, we have learned various insights and lessons from successful LLC owners. This section will address the key takeaways you can pick from the diverse insights learned by the legends and throughout this guidebook.

Extracting Nuggets of Wisdom

Nuggets of wisdom often come from people who have gone through an arduous journey, emerged on the other side, and lived to tell the tale (and have a few tips to improve that journey, too!). In business, these nuggets of wisdom can affect the company directly or indirectly. The following are nuggets we have lived by as entrepreneurs and still aim at making them our regular practice:

- Step out of your comfort zone and take more risks. You'll be surprised by the new experiences you will encounter.

- Eat well, exercise, and get enough sleep. Depriving yourself using unhealthy practices limits the mental and physical capacity you bring to the business.

- Be quick to appreciate and encourage your team for their outstanding work. It creates more loyalty and commitment to the company.

- Recognize high performance and nurture its growth while eliminating underperformance by addressing the points of weakness.

- If you think a task, idea, or challenge is hard, adjust your mindset, and you'll be surprised how your approach changes.

- Think through any business advice you receive; do not ignore your intuition and your personal experiences.

Applying Battle-Tested Best Practices to Your LLC

As the LLC leader, you assume all responsibility for your company's performance. Therefore, it is important to identify the best business practices for smooth operation, compliance, and a positive relationship between partners, employees, and clients. Here are some critical battle-tested practices to implement:

- Understand the basics of an LLC and implement the essential aspects

- Develop an operating agreement and use it as a reference for disputes

- Keep good and accurate financial records

- Comply with crucial state and federal-specific requirements

- Protect your LLC with favorable insurance coverage

- Take advantage of tax benefits and stay compliant

- Adapt to emerging changes and consider scaling upwards

Sidestepping Common Pitfalls with Confidence

Becoming a successful business owner is rewarding. But you must put in the hard work and avoid common pitfalls that may cause you to stagnate or close down your company. The following table shows the common pitfalls you may encounter and how to sidestep them.

Common Pitfall	How to Sidestep with Confidence
Forming LLC in the wrong state	Form the LLC in the state in which you plan to conduct business if you want to avoid DBA issues
Failing to separate personal and business finances	Form the LLC in the state in which you plan to conduct business if you want to avoid DBA issues
Having a weak operating agreement	Draft a detailed and dependable operating agreement to cater to arising LLC matters
Not consulting professionals	Talk to diverse professionals experienced in crucial areas in your LLC to help you cover all legal, financial, and tax grounds

From the onset, aim to build a strong foundation for your LLC business by avoiding these common pitfalls so that you can withstand any storms that may come your way.

Key Takeaways

- A key industry insight is to begin in a small way and keep costs down to avoid depending heavily on outside funding.

- Having a business idea and the passion to start a business is not enough. You must research vital strategies implemented by successful LLC owners and do the same or improve on them.

- Entrepreneurs with grit motivate themselves to move forward and learn from mistakes as they grow.

- Applying best business practices ensures your operations run smoothly, remain compliant, and have a healthy relationship with your partners, employees, and customers.

Chapter 11

Key Resources

> "Whenever you see a successful business, someone once made a courageous decision."
> -Peter Drucker

Legal and Business Resources

This section focuses on giving you the necessary resources to assist you in kickstarting your LLC. We shall provide helpful legal and government resources and explain how to establish a virtual office.

Online Legal Resources

- LLC (Limited Liability Company) - Start an LLC | LegalZoom: https://bit.ly/LegalZoomLLCGuide

- LLC Laws by State - LLC Statutes by State: https://howtostartanllc.com/llc-statute

- 50-State Guide to Forming an LLC | Nolo: https://bit.ly/50stateLLC

- LLC Annual Fees by State - All 50 States [2023 Costs] |

LLCU®: https://bit.ly/LLCbyState

- URS Agents | Registered Agent Services: https://bit.ly/LLCRegisteredAgent

- All 50 State Agencies That Issue Small Business Licenses and Permits: https://bit.ly/SmallBizLicense

- Best Small-Business Insurance 2023: Compare Options - NerdWallet: https://bit.ly/LLCSmallBizInsurance

Government Websites and Agencies

- Stay legally compliant | U.S. Small Business Administration: https://bit.ly/LegalComplianceLLC

- Apply for licenses and permits | U.S. Small Business Administration: https://bit.ly/LicenseAndPermitsLLC

- Your account | Internal Revenue Service (irs.gov): https://www.irs.gov/your-account

- New and Small Businesses | U.S. Department of Labor: https://bit.ly/DolLLC

- Apply for an Employer Identification Number (EIN) Online | Internal Revenue Service: https://bit.ly/EinAppLLC

- Trademarks | USPTO: Trademarks | USPTO:

Legal Forms and Templates

- 2022 Form 1040: https://www.irs.gov/pub/irs-pdf/f1040.pdf

- 2023 Form 1040-ES: https://www.irs.gov/pub/irs-pdf/f1040es.pdf

- 2023 Schedule C (Form 1040): https://www.irs.gov/pub/irs-pdf/f1040sc.pdf

- 2022 Schedule K-1 (Form 1041): https://www.irs.gov/pub/irs-pdf/f1041sk1.pdf

- 2022 Form 1065: https://www.irs.gov/pub/irs-pdf/f1065.pdf

- Free Business Plan Template with Examples (PDF): https://www.lawdistrict.com/business-plan/

- Free LLC Operating Agreement Template (US): https://www.lawdistrict.com/llc-operating-agreement/

- Free Multi-Member LLC Operating Agreement: https://www.lawdistrict.com/llc-operating-agreement/multi-member/

- Single Member LLC Operating Agreement - PDF: https://www.lawdistrict.com/llc-operating-agreement/single-member/

Setting up a virtual office/phone number for your LLC

As you start your LLC, you'll need a mailing address to include in your company's formation documents and a place to receive mail. If you don't have a commercial office space, you can use a PO Box or home address, but this is not the safest method. Besides, some states and local areas do not permit PO Box use. You can solve this challenge by acquiring a virtual address.

A virtual address allows you to use an actual street address as your company's virtual mailbox. This enables you to receive all important mail and protect your privacy. It also gives your business a professional image, as the mail center is usually in a commercial area. Most virtual offices also have phone numbers they can assign to your LLC and registered agents for receiving your documents. It's usually possible to set up mail forwarding to your home address as well.

Online Tools and Software

Starting a business in this day and age allows you to take advantage of advanced technology. You can automate various tasks and use software that limits human errors. Consider setting up the following tools in your LLC.

Accounting and Bookkeeping Tools

- Expensify | Spend Management Software for Receipts & Expenses: https://www.expensify.com/

- TurboTax® Official Site: File Taxes Online, Tax Filing Made Easy: https://turbotax.intuit.com/

- Simple Double-Entry Accounting For Your Business - FreshBooks: https://bit.ly/freshbooksLLC

- Best Online Accounting Software for your business in USA - Zoho Books: https://www.zoho.com/us/books/

- Oracle NetSuite: https://bit.ly/OracleForLLC

- Free Cloud Accounting Software | Odoo: https://bit.ly/OdooLLC

Project Management Software

- Zapier | Automation that moves you forward: https://zapier.com/

- Manage your team's work, projects, & tasks online • Asana: https://asana.com/

- Google Workspace: Secure Online Productivity & Collaboration Tools: https://workspace.google.com/

- Xodo Sign Free Trial (eversign.com): https://eversign.com/trial/docracy

- Where work happens | Slack: https://slack.com/

Marketing and SEO Tools

- Canva: Visual Suite for Everyone: https://www.canva.com/

- Kickstarter: https://www.kickstarter.com/

- Social Media Marketing and Management Tool: https://www.hootsuite.com/

- Analytics Tools & Solutions for Your Business - Google Analytics: https://marketingplatform.google.com/about/analytics/

- Free Tools | HubSpot: https://www.hubspot.com

- Marketing, Automation & Email Platform | Mailchimp: https://mailchimp.com/

Communication and Collaboration Tools

- OpenPhone | Modern business phone for startups and small businesses: https://www.openphone.com/

- 10 BEST Virtual Address for Business & Mailbox Services (2023): https://www.guru99.com/best-virtual-mailbox-service.html

- Collaboration Tools and Solutions for Business | Teams: https://www.microsoft.com/en-us/microsoft-teams/collaboration

- Online Whiteboard for Team Collaboration | Miro: https://bit.ly/LLCCollab

- Confluence - Team Collaboration Software | Atlassian: https://bit.ly/AtLassLLC

Internalizing the Entrepreneurial Mindset

Before we wrap up here, we're going to give you a few mindset-oriented tips that every entrepreneur should know.

Starting and growing a business is a journey. There will be ups and downs, and your ability to navigate those with a clear head will determine whether or not you succeed in the long run.

So as you embark on this journey, remember the following:

Even Keel is the Way to Go

You'll have a myriad of wins and losses as an entrepreneur. The key is to not get too high during the wins, or too low during the losses. The better you can manage your emotions through the ups and downs, the more consistently you'll perform, and the better off your business will be.

Of course, this is easier said than done.

Here's a few tips on managing your emotions:

- Make sure you sleep 7-8 hours every night, in a dark cold room.

- Whenever you feel stressed, take a few minutes and focus on your breath. Breathe deeply, count to five on the inhale, exhale, and hold in between. This will calm you down and ground you.

- Eat healthy. Your mental state is a reflection of what you consume and put into your body. If that's a ton of processed junk food, you'll find it exceedingly hard to feel good and manage your emotions. On the other hand, if you eat clean and healthy and limit the junk food, you'll have more clarity and a better emotional baseline.

- Take time off. We recommend taking at least one day off each week where you do nothing business-related. This will help you reset, unwind, and mentally prepare yourself for the week of work. It'll also help you avoid bouts of burnout, which can set you back weeks.

- Have a fitness routine. Whether it be walking, hitting the gym, or playing a sport - moving your body consistently is great for mental health.

- Limit alcohol consumption. There's no way around it - when you push your limits in business, you often operate at your edge. Drinking, even a little bit, can tip you over that edge and set you back in a big way. Especially during periods of intense work, it's a good idea to limit alcohol intake.

Contribution Breaks the Curse

We've had a few lows on our business journey. For example, early on in a coaching business of ours, we hit a rough month of sales, where after averaging $50-100k in revenue monthly, there was a dry patch with no sales for a three-week span.

It was one of those periods where it felt like we'd never see a sale roll in again. Coaching applications were drying up, hardly anyone was scheduling calls, and it felt like our leads were more unqualified than ever.

Instead of going down with the ship and freaking out, we decided to take massive action. We hit the pavement and started making tons of lead-generating content on YouTube, Instagram, and TikTok.

Within a few weeks, the curse was indeed broken. We managed to hit $50k in sales that month, and followed it up with a record-breaking month the following month.

Taking action will make you feel better, and as a result you'll show up to clients and prospects better. Additionally, it'll set the stage to bring in more leads and create more business in the short and long term.

Offense vs Defense

Most people live their lives perpetually on defense. They take very few risks, and as a result, don't typically reap big rewards.

But if you want to build a thriving business, you've got to get used to playing offense. Sure, there's a time and place for defense and being in "protection mode." But if you don't play offense and shift into an "attack mode" mentality, you won't have much to protect in the first place.

Have a Solution-Focused Approach

With a solution-focused approach, you focus on solving the problems that come up, rather than being hyper-focused on the problems themselves (and having a freak-out, like many people do).

This allows you to stay calm, cool, and collected, and generate solutions that help you to maintain and grow your business.

Conclusion

An LLC is one of the best structures to choose as you start your business journey. Even though it has vital legal and financial implications, the benefits outweigh the responsibilities. The process may appear complicated and even scary in the beginning. However, this guidebook has given you the core requirements and best practices for properly setting up and running an LLC.

At this point, you have probably figured out why it would be best to choose an LLC instead of some other legal entity, such as a greater level of personal liability protection and taxation flexibility. In addition, you got a step-by-step guide on the formation process, including selecting a company name, hiring a registered agent to file your articles of organization, and drafting an operating agreement. You also learned of the ongoing maintenance requirements, such as holding members' meetings, submitting annual reports, and staying compliant.

Even though every state has its own LLC regulations, this guidebook has outlined general aspects that all LLC founders in whichever state can apply. If you use the information provided within every page of this book, you will have the ability to fulfill all federal, state, and local obligations, as well as open business accounts, obtain an EIN, and purchase necessary insurance policies.

You also have the legal and government resources you need to start working on your LLC at your disposal. Not only that, but we have also outlined marketing, accounting, and project management tools that will assist you in performing some tasks from the onset, which will help you treamline everything.

Along the way, you might face the complex legal situations involved in scaling your business, bringing additional investors, mergers and acquisitions, or expanding beyond the state limits. When that time comes, you should talk with business lawyers and financial advisors as you work on amending your operating agreements. Even at this point, this guidebook has provided you with reliable information that can help you know what action to take.

But for now, you are armed with the knowledge you need to start your LLC confidently. The administrative duties may seem cumbersome, but you understand exactly what it takes to comply. The most important thing is that your business has proper legal support and structure that makes it possible for you to develop a successful, profitable business in due time.

Starting an LLC is the road less traveled, and it has its ups and downs, but remember, your dreams are worth the investment of time and resources. Remain committed to your vision, but be flexible along the way. Surround yourself with people who share your aspiration to build a successful business. There will be trials, yet it is these challenges that propel you forward when you overcome them. What lies behind doesn't compare to the bold future you are building. You are strong; therefore, dream big and allow the inside adventurer in you to come alive. Congratulations on taking these important first steps, and best of luck executing your vision within a stable, smart LLC entity designed for long-term growth.

Your Next Step

As a way of saying thank you for your purchase, we're offering three FREE downloads that are exclusive to our book readers!

- The Start Your LLC Checklist

- The 5 Mistakes Beginners Make When Opening an LLC

- The 7 Best Websites for Starting Your LLC

Inside all these bonuses, you'll discover:

- The top 3 states to start your LLC to give it the best chance of success, and most tax advantages.

- All your LLC questions answered so you can get it going with zero confusion.

- The top 7 websites to start your LLC ranked, with pros and cons for each, so you can easily choose the best one for your situation.

- The #1 mistake beginners make that can doom your LLC before you even make your first sale (and how to avoid it).

- All this, and much more…

To download your bonuses, you can go to www.LLCLegend.com or simply scan the QR code below!

Can You Do Us a Favor?

Thanks for checking out our book.

We're confident this will help you build your LLC and create a thriving business!

Would you take 60 seconds and write a quick blurb about this book on Amazon?

Reviews are the best way for independent authors (like us) to get noticed, sell more books, and spread our message to as many people as possible. We also read every review and use the feedback to write future revisions – and future books, even.

To leave your review, just visit: https://amzn.to/49iXcpi

Or scan this QR code:

Thank you – we really appreciate your support.

About the Author

Garrett Monroe is a pen name for a team of writers with business experience in various industries, like coaching, sales, AI, real estate, copywriting, accounting, etc. They've built teams, understand how to manage people, and know what it takes to be a successful entrepreneur. These writers have come together to share their knowledge and produce a series of business books and help you take your business endeavors to the next level.

References

1. Corporation Requirements: Everything You Need to Know. (n.d.). UpCounsel. https://www.upcounsel.com/corporation-requirements#:~:text=These%20continuous%20requirements%20include%20those%20related%20to%20the,. . .%206%20State%20registration. %20. . .%207%20Licensing. %20

2. What is an operating agreement? Do I need one for my LLC? (2023, November 9). Thomson Reuters Legal. https://legal.thomsonreuters.com/en/insights/articles/what-is-an-operating-agreement

3. Tarver, E. (2023, November 1). Market segmentation: definition, example, types, benefits. Investopedia. https://www.investopedia.com/terms/m/marketsegmentation.asp

4. Business compliance requirements & consequences. (2021, January 26). https://www.wolterskluwer.com/en/expert-insights/business-compliance-requirements-and-consequences

5. Having an LLC in multiple states. (n.d.). https://formationscorp.com/blog/having-an-llc-in-multiple-states

6. How to apply for an EIN | Internal Revenue Service. (n.d.). https://www.irs.gov/businesses/small-businesses-self-employed/how-to-apply-for-an-ein

7. Staff, C. (2023, December 1). Conflict Management: Definition, Strategies, and Styles. Coursera. https://www.coursera.org/articles/conflict-management

8. Apply for licenses and permits. (n.d.). U.S. Small Business Administration. https://www.sba.gov/business-guide/launch-your-business/apply-licenses-permits

9. McCullah, S. (2022b, April 4). Debt financing vs. equity financing: Do you want to take out a loan or take on investors? Business Insider. https://www.businessinsider.com/personal-finance/debt-financing-vs-equity-financing

10. 4 Examples of business negotiation Strategies | HBS Online. (2023, June 15). Business Insights Blog. https://online.hbs.edu/blog/post/negotiating-in-business

11. Collaboration and Partnership: How to build strong alliances for business success. (n.d.). https://www.strategicadvisorboard.com/blog-posts/collaboration-and-partnership-how-to-build-strong-alliances-for-business-success#:~:text=Steps%20to%20Building%20Strong%20Alliances%201%201.%20Define,communication%20plan%20. . .%206%206.%20Manage%20the%20partnership

12. Robinson, A. (2022, November 30). 14 Crucial HR skills, Competencies & qualifications. teambuilding.com. https://teambuilding.com/blog/hr-skills

13. Abhi, T. P. (2023, December 13). Brand Protection 101: Ensuring the security of your brand online. Promote Abhi. https://www.promoteabhi.com/blog/brand-protection-guide

14. Indeed Editorial Team. "10 Types of Business Risks and How to Manage Them." Indeed Career Guide, www.indeed.com/career-advice/starting-new-job/types-of-business-risk

15. 5 Common Misconceptions about the R&D Tax Credit—and Whether You Qualify. (2021, March 12). https://www.mossadams.com/articles/2021/03/company-qualifications-for-the-r-d-tax-credit

16. eMoney Advisor. (2023, December 7). Creating a Financial Advisor Business Plan: A Comprehensive guide. https://emoneyadvisor.com/blog/creating-a-financial-advisor-business-plan-a-comprehensive-guide/

17. deloitteeditor. (2021, March 13). Leaving a legacy for your company, your team, and yourself. WSJ. https://deloitte.wsj.com/cfo/leaving-a-legacy-for-your-company-your-team-and-yourself-01552435330

18. Feldman, S. (2024, July 31). How to close an LLC: Dissolution, winding up, and termination. https://www.wolterskluwer.com/en/expert-insights/dissolving-winding-up-and-terminating-a-limited-liability-company?

19. Petersen, R. (2021, June 19). 15 inspiring case studies of pivoting. BarnRaisers, LLC. https://barnraisersllc.com/2021/06/19/15-inspiring-case-studies-of-pivoting/

20. Todd, D. (2021, December 30). Passion, grit, resilience: the formula for success. Entrepreneur. https://www.entrepreneur.com/leadership/passion-grit-resilience-the-formula-for-success/

Printed in Great Britain
by Amazon

42021335R00096